Conflict and
Resolution

CONFLICT AND RESOLUTION

Barbara A. Nagle-Lechman
Associate Professor
Montclair State University

Aspen Law & Business
A Division of Aspen Publishers, Inc.

ISBN 1-56706-4787

This publication is designed to provide accurate and authoritative information in regard to the subject matter covered. It is sold with the understanding that the publisher is not engaged in rendering legal, accounting, or other professional services. If legal advice or other professional assistance is required, the services of a competent professional person should be sought.

> — From a *Declaration of Principles* jointly adopted by a Committee of the American Bar Association and a Committee of Publishers and Associations.

Permissions
Aspen Law & Business
A Division of Aspen Publishers, Inc.,
1185 Avenue of the Americas
New York, NY 10036

2 3 4 5

Printed in the United States of America

Library of Congress Cataloging-in-Publication Data

Nagle-Lechman, Barbara A., 1944–
    Conflict and resolution / Barbara A. Nagle-Lechman.
        p.   cm.
    Includes bibliographical references and index.
    ISBN 1-56706-478-7
    1. Dispute resolution (Law) — United States.   2. Arbitration and award — United States.   3. Mediation — United States.   4. Negotiation.   5. Conflict management.   I. Title.
    KF9084.N35   1997
    347.73'9 — dc21   97-20103
                                                                  CIP

Summary of Contents

Contents

1. Introduction   1

2. Conflict 15

3. Negotiation 33

Mediation 61

5. Arbitration 97

6. Other Forms of Dispute Resolution   113

7. Policy, Ethical, and Practice Issues   133

Appendices

Preface

The goal of this book is to provide paralegal and legal assistant students with an understanding of conflict and a working knowledge of the three major forms of dispute resolution in the legal field — negotiation, mediation, and arbitration. It is my hope that students will apply the theory and practice of dispute resolution to their personal as well as their professional lives.

The first two chapters concern the nature and diverse sources of authority, and offer an overview of conflict resolution processes. Then, in chapters 3-5, more careful consideration is given to negotiation, mediation, and arbitration, respectively. The last two chapters serve as an introduction to other forms of dispute resolution in the legal context and to selected policy and ethical issues in the field. Each chapter concludes with a summary and exercises designed to engage students in knowledge application, integration, and expansion. Some chapters include role plays to allow students to experience how the theories of dispute resolution are practiced.

There are a number of ways this book can be used. It has served as the basic text in an undergraduate legal studies course. It could also be used in a section of a civil litigation course or of an introductory law course. Finally, it could be the basis of a unit on dispute resolution in a course of study for paralegals.

I would like to thank my colleagues and teachers at the Hewlitt Institute for Socio-Legal Dispute Resolution at The Ohio State University in 1993, several of whom read preliminary drafts: Carol King, Tom Grexa, and Theresa Hagen. I would also like to thank friends and colleagues closer to home who have looked at drafts and made suggestions: Joseph Ryan, Rosalie Cannone McGill, Sheila O'Shea, Marilyn Tayler, and my pastor, Rev. Dorcas Dias-Shaner for our "writing group." My students at Montclair State University have been a great source of inspiration and continue to teach me and improve my teaching in this field. My graduate assistant Rich Adams, and several students who worked with me at various stages in the process, Viki Giammarella and Dina Sadik, all contributed to the final product. The individual who contributed the most to the production of this book is a former student and now a colleague, attorney and adjunct professor Louis A. Chiafullo. Finally, I want to thank my husband, George Lechman, who always helps me experience conflict and its resolution from a very personal perspective and who provides ongoing support in so many ways that make life beautiful.

Barbara Nagle-Lechman

March 1997

Acknowledgments

The author gratefully acknowledges the permissions granted to reproduce the following materials:

Bush, Robert A. Baruch, *The Dilemmas of Mediation Practice: A Study of Ethical Dilemmas and Policy Implications* (1992). National Institute for Dispute Resolution, Washington. Reprinted with permission.

Code of Ethics for Arbitrators in Commercial Disputes (1977). American Arbitration Association and American Bar Association. Reprinted with permission.

Goldberg, Stephen B., Sander, Frank E. A., & Rogers, Nancy H., *Dispute Resolution: Negotiation, Mediation, and Other Processes,* pages 72, 148-155, 223-224, 226-227, 230, 235, 251, 291 (2nd ed. 1992). Copyright © 1992 by Little, Brown & Company, assigned to Aspen Law & Business, a division of Aspen Publishers, Inc. Reprinted with permission.

Leeson, Susan M. & Johnston, Bryan M. *Ending It: Dispute Resolution in America* (1988). © 1988 by Anderson Publishing Co. Reprinted with permission.

McIver, John P. & Keilitz, Susan, Court-Annexed Arbitration: An Introduction, 13 Justice Sys. J. 123 (1991). Reprinted with permission.

Model Standards of Conduct for Mediators (1994). American Arbitration Association, American Bar Association, and Society of Professionals in Dispute Resolution. Reprinted with permission.

Murray, John S., *Process of Dispute Resolution: The Role of Lawyers* (1989). Reprinted with permission by Foundation Press, Inc., Westbury, New York.

Raiffa, Howard, *The Art and Science of Negotiation* (1981). Copyright © 1981 by the President and Fellows of Harvard College. Reprinted by permission of Harvard University Press.

Sander, Frank E. A., The Courthouse and Alternative Dispute Resolution, reprinted in *Negotiation Strategies for Mutual Gain: The Basic Seminar of the Program on Negotiation at Harvard Law School* (Lavinia Hall, ed. 1993). SAGE Publications, Inc., Newbury Park. Reprinted with permission.

Scott, Gini Graham, *Resolving Conflict* (1990). Reprinted with permission by New Harbinger Publications, Oakland, California.

Singer, Linda R., *Settling Disputes: Conflict Resolution in Business, Families, and The Legal System* (2d ed. 1994). Copyright © 1994 by Westview Press. Reprinted by permission of Westview Press.

Worchel, Stephen & Simpson, Jeffrey A., eds., *Conflict Between People & Groups* (1993). Nelson Hall, Chicago. Reprinted with permission.

Conflict and
Resolution

Introduction

Introductory Notes

Conflict's Impact and the Necessity of Understanding Conflict
>   Conflict Is Pervasive
>   Reaction to Conflict
>   Sources of Conflict

Overview of Conflict Resolution Processes
>   Negotiation
>   Mediation
>   Arbitration
>   Other Processes
>   The Court System

Exercises

Jennifer Rose and Charles Finnery have been partners in the practice of law for eight years. In the beginning it appeared that their talents complemented one another. Jennifer was the litigator and the person who brought in most of the business. Charles took care of the office management and did residential real estate, trusts and estates work, and some small corporate work. They never entered into a formal partnership agreement because they were friends before they started the partnership. For the past five years, you have worked as their paralegal and really enjoy the variety of work, the relaxed way they run their office, and the flexible working schedule they permit you to follow.

For the last six months, however, things have been tense in the office and are getting increasingly worse. You don't know the source of the problem, but both Charles and Jennifer are miserable and it is rubbing off on you. Sometimes they explode into shouting matches and name-calling, which you find very unprofessional. You know from doing the bookkeeping that income is down and you think it may be due to the present situation. Things have gotten so bad that you have considered quitting. Even if you stay, the partnership may break up and neither attorney could afford you on their own. The truth is you like Jennifer and Charles a great deal and it saddens you to see what is happening. . . . It's almost like a divorce!

Can you suggest anything to help Jennifer and Charles through their present struggle? You don't want to get caught in the middle, but you do want things to return to the way they were before this conflict started. What can you do?

Introductory Notes

This book explores conflicts like the foregoing as well as a variety of others; it considers how they develop, how they affect the parties in conflict as well as society at large, and how conflict resolution processes[1] and our legal system respond to them. The goal is to enable readers to understand and accept conflict in their own lives, in their communities, in the legal environment, and in the larger global context. Then, the readers are introduced to a number of conflict resolution theories and techniques so that they can understand and, in some cases, be able to apply those techniques. The final goal is to enable individuals to understand and be prepared to participate in the processes in which conflicts and disputes are managed and resolved.

Because this book is written for undergraduate and graduate Legal Studies students, the nature of conflict and its resolution is presented from a legal perspective: its impact on attorneys, legal assistants, and other legal specialists is highlighted throughout the text. The reader should bear in mind that there are diverse approaches to this subject. Alternate dispute resolution (ADR) is very much a part of the legal landscape today, and it is imperative that paralegals be familiar with the ADR processes available in their jurisdiction.

---

1. Throughout the court system, these processes are frequently referred to as *alternate dispute resolution* (ADR). In some jurisdictions, such as New Jersey, they are called *complementary dispute resolution*. They are often simply referred to as *dispute resolution*.

The model of conflict and its resolution that is developed here is the one that permeates the dominant culture in the United States. This has been called the "European Model." While a consideration of other techniques and systems is beyond the scope of this book, one needs to be aware that there are other conflict resolution models both in the United States and throughout the world that justify further study. Cultural differences also influence conflict, and conflict resolution that takes account of such diversity is discussed briefly at pages 23-25.

Conflict's Impact and the Necessity of Understanding Conflict

Conflict Is Pervasive

Individuals and groups are faced with conflict from the beginning of life to its end. A baby cries because it wants something, but the baby's parents do not always know what the infant wants. This conflict arises from the inability to communicate effectively. A youth wants to play with her friends instead of doing homework. There is a conflict between the youth and her parent as a result of differing values. A young adult wishes to continue her education beyond an undergraduate degree and seeks parental support. While the parents may want to help their daughter, financial constraints prohibit it. An adult may want to enter into a second marriage against the wishes of the children. Conflict arises in employment situations regarding salary, working conditions, personnel, and related issues. An elderly person may wish to continue to live independently, while the children fear for his safety and security if such independent living continues. Purchasers and sellers of houses, autos, and other significant items frequently disagree on the value of such items.

A group of individuals — bound together by the commitment to common values — may clash with other groups espousing different values over such issues as abortion, free speech, entitlements, and gun control. It sometimes appears that, as a nation, we are divided among racial, ethnic, gender, class, economic, and creedal lines.

Companies and similar organizations are also conflicted. They enter into contracts that may result in an unsatisfactory relationship, creating a dispute between the parties to the contract. There may be conflicts between subdivisions of an organization resulting from a disagreement over territory or resources, such as departments within a school vying for limited funds. There are conflicts within organizations over management policies. Conflicts also arise when employees or groups of employees believe they should receive greater compensation or more extensive benefits and the employer does not agree.

Labor union agreements have traditionally included hearings, arbitration, or mediation as a system for dispute resolution. Employer/employee conflicts in the private sector are resolved through grievance procedures and ADR processes governed largely by labor union contracts. While the early part of this century saw the rise of private sector labor contracts, the latter part of this century has shown a significant decline of unionization in the private sector with the growth of unionization in the public sector. However, both the means to reach agreement as well as the application of agreements continue to require the dispute resolution methods considered here.

Government, in all of its manifestations, is also faced with daily conflict. Elections are a result, at least in part, of conflicting ideas. Different branches of government have different agendas, giving rise to adverse interests. State and county governments may disagree on which of them is financially responsible for the court system. A shortage of resources can contribute to such disputes. Nations find themselves faced with seemingly insurmountable disputes both within their borders and with other nations.

In the United States, we are very litigious. This means, among other things, that we take many of our conflicts to courts of law for resolution. While a vast majority of lawsuits are settled out of court prior to trial, the reason a plaintiff brings a lawsuit is to seek the court's intervention and ultimate rendering of a decision regarding the dispute.

Reaction to Conflict

It is clear that conflict cannot be avoided. In fact, conflict probably should not be avoided entirely; it can have beneficial results and be viewed as an opportunity for enhanced communication and positive change. Conflict needs to be recognized, understood, and managed or resolved.

A list of conflicts and potential conflicts can be endless, and people in the United States tend to deal with conflicts in a variety of ways. The first, at one end of a continuum, is conflict avoidance. While some might believe this to be a laudatory goal, it is probably not possible for any individual to achieve and, as stated above, it may not be psychologically healthy. Similarly, avoidance is not an appropriate business practice for a company.

The next technique to note along the continuum is suppression. Here, while the disagreement is understood to exist, neither party is willing to face it, or one party is willing to "lump it" — i.e., swallow her pride and let the other have his way. This can arise from a culture that promotes such a response, from a fear of confrontation and anger, or from an attitude that life is too short to engage in every conflict. For example, some people confront strangers who use racially offensive language, while others swallow their anger and try to disengage themselves from that person.

At the other end of the continuum is violence. One of the reasons for the interference of the courts in the lives of individuals is to provide a solution to conflict that avoids violence. A person's reaction to conflict will vary with the type of conflict faced, such as a professional disagreement versus a gang war, as well as the skills each individual has developed to deal with conflict.

Once a conflict develops into a dispute recognizable as one for which our judicial system may provide a remedy, there can be another whole series of dispute resolution methods. The most recognized is "taking him to court," also known as "I'll see you in court." Before the conflicting parties make it to court, however, they sometimes choose or are directed to participate in one of the dispute resolution processes that are the subject of this book. The movement encouraging the use of these processes has a number of sources and rationales, including an expansion of individual rights, the expense of litigation, and the effort to empower people to participate in the resolution of their own disputes.

No one resolution method is the answer to all conflicts. There is no panacea. However, each method or some combination of them may play a necessary role in each dispute. Their use may be further dictated by considerations of time, resources, relational impact, nature of the parties, and the nature of the conflict.

Sources of Conflict

While it is tempting to lay responsibility for conflict at the feet of one significant instigator, it is clear that conflict arises in a variety of situations, in distinctive configurations, and from different sources. It is likely that one's background and experience will influence one's perception as to the real source of conflict. Readers may find some overlap in the following discussion regarding sources of conflict and may disagree. The point is that the source of conflict must be critically examined before a responsive strategy can be developed.

A major source of misunderstandings that lead to conflict is communication breakdown due to ineffective communication patterns. If parties cannot communicate, or do not understand one another, it is unlikely that they will be able to resolve differences or "work out their problems." An indicator of the pervasiveness of this problem is that mediation training invariably directs neutrals to aid the parties in improving their ability to communicate with one another.

Another significant contributor to conflict is a power imbalance between the parties, which is taken advantage of by the more powerful one. If one of the parties is more powerful, she is in a position to require the other to comply with her will. This more powerful party may be an individual, an organization, or a country. Such an exercise of power will likely anger and frustrate the less powerful party, and the more powerful disputant will lose respect for the weaker one. Additionally, the blatant exercise of power by one party over the other can leave the weaker party waiting for the next opportunity to even the score. Again, the mediation literature speaks of the need to be sensitive to the balance of power between disputing parties.

Power shifts during a relationship are similarly causative. For example, if a husband had previously been the major provider of the family income and decides, or is forced, to stay home and care for the family because the wife lands a better job, power within the family may shift and cause marital difficulty. Similarly, in the work environment, if a professional is promoted and made supervisor of her previous peers, power has shifted and will likely cause conflict.

Economics influence conflict in various ways. If the parties have different economic resources, it can create a power imbalance. If there are insufficient resources, parties will fight over the limited resources available. Biases are sometimes built upon economic differences and may result in a perception of differing values. One party may be jealous of another's financial success, resulting in friction between them. If paralegals in the same firm are paid differing salaries, even though they do similar work and have similar experience levels, conflict will result.

Divergent values between individuals, organizations and groups, and nations and cultures can contribute to the disruption of harmony. One must be aware, however, that the claim of differing values is sometimes used to conceal unexpressed pecuniary or emotional interests that may be at the heart of the dispute. Conflicts that do arise from value differences sometimes result in the parties disputing over a "matter of principle." When this happens, attempts to have them reach a satisfactory compromise are difficult. However, if each party understands that the conflict arises from divergent value systems, they may be more empathic toward each other and more able to manage the conflict.

Out of a desire for comfort and similarity, individuals, groups, and sovereigns distance themselves from others whose values they perceive to be different. This can lead to misunderstanding, poor communication, and other conflict instigators. Racial, ethnic, and cultural differences must be considered. Stereotyping, however, encourages disputants and neutrals to overlook the individual and perceive only generalized attributes. Such behavior is unlikely to contribute to conflict resolution and may actually contribute to the conflict.

A less significant but important contributor to conflict is the differing experience levels of the participants. While it is foolish to tout experience as the precursor to wisdom, experience can and should contribute to knowledge and a broader problem-solving resource base. Inexperience, on the other hand, may actually result in a more creative approach. Parties with different levels of experience need to remain open to the other and maintain mutual respect.

Disputants' sensitivity levels can be placed on a continuum, both extremes being factors that contribute to conflict problems. On one end are the insensitive parties. These are people who are totally unconcerned with anyone other than themselves. On the other end are the parties who are overly sensitive and believe that whatever is said is directed at them. Such attributes interfere with productive communication and relationship maintenance.

A dispute or conflict begins on one level but rarely remains there. Conflicts can dissipate or escalate. Escalation occurs, either over the original problem, over the process utilized to resolve it, or due to the insensitivity of one party to the existence of the conflict. Parties personalize communications and become entrenched in their positions. Therefore, students of conflict must be aware of the stage of escalation the conflict has reached to better understand the parties and their dispute.

Another source of conflict is societal change. Historically, religious leaders, precepts of a given faith, respect for the guidance of elders or family members, and social mores were factors that ensured conflict avoidance and resolution. Those who "played by the rules" had a measure of predictability as to the outcome of their actions. With the change of family, religious, and social structure, individuality has replaced conformity and uncertainty has replaced predictability.

Finally, what appears to be the immediate or current conflict may just be the top layer. If parties have had previous conflicts, one or both may be angry over a previous wrong, may have suppressed their anger when that wrong occurred, and may now be "getting even." The party may then be less likely to engage in conflict resolution or less likely to trust the other party. Simply resolving the surface problem is unlikely to keep the parties out of future conflicts.

This by no means exhausts the list of the origins of conflict; it is meant to lead the reader into considering other sources. Understanding the source of a particular conflict can contribute to its effective management and resolution. Frequently, the problem is not what appears on the surface, but another conflict of an ongoing nature which is below the surface and not spoken.

Overview of Conflict Resolution Processes

Negotiation

The form of conflict resolution that most people practice throughout life is negotiation. When one person wants something and another does not want to give it to him, the two people negotiate. A young child who wants candy negotiates with a parent to obtain the sweet. The teen who wants certain privileges negotiates with the parent for those privileges. A student who believes she earned a higher grade than the one she received may negotiate with the professor to raise the grade. A legal assistant negotiates with a vendor regarding services provided to the law firm.

Black's Law Dictionary (6th ed. 1990) defines "negotiation" as "[t]he deliberation, discussions, or conference upon the terms of a proposed agreement; the act of settling or arranging the terms and conditions of a bargain, sale, or other business transaction." In negotiation, a person either represents himself or is represented by an advocate or an agent, frequently over an extended period of time and a number of meetings or communications. Theoretically, the give-and-take process of negotiation between the parties leads to a resolution that is acceptable to both parties. Sometimes a resolution does not result.

Unlike most of the other forms of conflict resolution, negotiation does not involve the participation of a third-party neutral. It is usually voluntary and participatory. It can occur in a formal or informal setting and can be done in person, by telephone, or through written communication. Most people have participated in some form of negotiation, either legal or nonlegal, and have developed some negotiation style.

Paralegals practice negotiation both from a personal and a professional perspective. They may negotiate salary, benefits, working conditions, office locations, support personnel, and job assignments. A paralegal is not expected, nor permitted, to negotiate a contract or a personal injury settlement on behalf of a client of the law firm. However, a paralegal who works as an advocate in social security matters may negotiate on behalf of the client, a paralegal manager in a large legal environment will negotiate with other office personnel, and a law office manager will negotiate with providers of services to the law office.

Much of what an attorney does revolves around the negotiation process. On any given day, an attorney may find herself negotiating with an adversary about an offer of settlement, negotiating with a client regarding how to proceed with a given matter, negotiating with court personnel over the scheduling of a hearing, and negotiating with a secretary about work priorities. For many years, attorneys were not trained in the art and science of negotiation. However, most law schools now recognize the need for skill development in this area.

Mediation

Mediation utilizes the skills of a third-party neutral. A third-party neutral is a person, or sometimes a panel of people, who is not involved in the dispute but participates in the process designed to reach a solution. In the mediation process, the third-party neutral, also known as the mediator, does not so much determine the outcome of the conflict as assists the disputing parties in reaching their own resolution. The mediator is, among other things, a facilitator rather than a judge. Mediation has been called "guided negotiation."

While mediation is less familiar to the layperson than negotiation, examples of it can be found outside the legal process. For instance, conflicted parties sometimes seek the assistance of a religious leader to help them work through their difficulties. In families, a senior member of the family may be sought out for her guidance in settling a conflict. In some homogeneous communities, a well-respected elder may be asked to resolve a dispute within the community. Sometimes these dispute resolutions take the form of arbitration, where the neutral renders a decision settling the matter. At other times, however, the neutral assists the parties in fashioning their own settlement. These are forms of mediation.

It is unlikely that paralegals will be called upon to serve as mediators in the law office. There are, however, opportunities for laypeople to serve as mediators, either as volunteers within their community or as compensated professionals. Programs that utilize the abilities of trained mediators can be found across the country. For example, a community-based program will train and supervise laypeople to serve as mediators in community disputes. Some college campuses train residence assistants in mediation and provide peer-mediation to aid in the resolution of conflicts between students.

In addition, paralegals in a law firm or governmental agency may prepare cases and witnesses for mediation in the same manner as they prepare cases for trial. And some paralegals are employed in administrative positions in mediation programs. For example, a paralegal may work in a court clerk's office and function as the mediation administrator/supervisor. It is important, therefore, to understand the process and its application. Most importantly, the communication skills that one develops as a result of mediation training contribute to expanded interpersonal competence and can be utilized in many situations.

Attorneys are involved in mediation in several ways. They represent their clients in a mediation process; they may provide for mediation or other dispute resolution process in a contract they are preparing for a client; they may recommend that a client utilize mediation services; or they may serve as mediators themselves. Some attorneys receive mediation training in law school, while others acquire the skills through private or court-annexed dispute resolution training.

Mediation can take place either privately or under the auspices of the courts. When it is under the direction of the court, a judge may refer disputants to a private mediator or may direct parties to participate in mediation at the courthouse. In many jurisdictions, court-annexed mediators must meet minimum educational or training requirements. Non-attorneys are actively involved in mediation as well, and there are almost no licensing or educational requirements for private mediators. There are particular areas of mediation practice in which both attorneys and mental health professionals share the arena, i.e., divorce and custody mediation.

Arbitration

Arbitration has a long and distinguished history in certain areas of conflict, e.g., labor and commercial disputes. Arbitration is a conflict resolution process that, like mediation, utilizes the services of a third-party neutral. It is very different, however, from mediation. Arbitration is a more intrusive process, in which the arbitrator holds a hearing and makes an award. It is similar in nature to a trial, except it is generally held in a more informal environment and is not bound by many of the requirements[2] that a court of law is obliged to follow. Arbitrators may be attor-

---

2. Such requirements usually proceed from the particular state's Rules of Evidence.

neys, but it is equally likely that an arbitrator is a specialist in a given field, such as construction or education.

A paralegal's work in arbitration includes preparing cases for arbitration, researching arbitration awards, researching contract law and preparing arbitration clauses for insertion into a contract, and sometimes attending an arbitration hearing. Paralegals do not themselves serve as arbitrators unless they have a particular expertise that qualifies them to do so. However, they might find themselves participating as a party in a court-annexed arbitration program.[3]

Attorneys frequently serve as arbitrators, particularly in commercial arbitration. They also prepare cases for arbitration and represent a client at an arbitration hearing. Attorneys may feel more comfortable with arbitration rather than mediation because arbitration is an adjudicatory process that enables them to exercise their adversarial skills.

Like mediation, arbitration can be found in the courts as well as the private sector. Court-annexed arbitration has grown in the last ten years. Yet private arbitration outside of the court system remains an attractive option for some disputants, and there are a number of organizations that are active in the private arbitration field. The American Arbitration Association (AAA) and Center for Public Resources, Inc. (CPR) are two examples. Arbitration training, both initial and advanced, is available through a variety of sources. As in mediation, there is presently no licensing or credentialing requirement for arbitrators imposed by the state. Each private sponsoring organization has its own qualifying requirements.

Other Processes

There are other conflict resolution processes available to disputants, both in the court and privately. Many are hybrids or derivations of the procedures named above. They are less pervasive than the three primary processes and are discussed in chapter 6.

The Court System

Many disputants take their conflict to the court system for resolution. It remains the primary dispute resolution forum utilized by attor-

---

3. When a disputant files a court action (i.e., a complaint) to commence litigation, some jurisdictions require the disputants to appear before an arbitrator who will hear their cases and make a binding, or more frequently, nonbinding award.

neys. Because each state, as well as the federal government, has its own court system, it is incumbent on the paralegal to be completely familiar with the particular state and federal court system and its practices.[4]

When neighbors fight over a barking dog, one of them will frequently file a complaint[5] in the town or municipal court. If a landlord wants to remove a tenant for failure to pay rent, she will file a complaint in the court that handles landlord/tenant matters. Liability for automobile accidents is usually decided in court. Criminal matters are brought to court by the state on behalf of the injured party. Contract actions, divorce, adoption, negligence, and many other judicially recognized conflicts find their way through our court system each year.

In addition to the trial level, where each party presents her case and the matter is decided by a judge or jury, there is an appellate procedure. This permits certain parties who are not satisfied with the trial court's determination to ask a higher court to review the matter based upon certain prescribed requirements, such as an error of law made by the trial judge.

However, even within the court system, as mandated by the Federal Rules of Civil Procedure, there is a requirement of a good faith attempt to settle the dispute.[6] Most cases do in fact settle before the actual trial or, as lawyers put it, "on the courthouse steps," and some settle after trial pending appeal. While the judicial system is a dispute resolution system, it will not be studied in depth here because our intent is to review those methods that are an alternative to or complement the court system.

EXERCISES

1. Itemize the conflicts you have had in your life in the past week, whether with individuals, businesses, the government, or similar entities. Next to each conflict indicate what you believe to be the cause and how it was managed.

2. Choose three current conflicts — one on a local level, one on a national level, and the third on an international level. Follow each in the media and track its progress.

---

4. The federal and state court systems and the practice within each is beyond the scope of this book but should be the subject of at least one course within the paralegal student's course of study.

5. "Filing a complaint" is the manner in which one commences a lawsuit and seeks the intervention of the formal court system.

6. Fed. R. Civ. P. 68.

3. List work-related issues a paralegal might negotiate, in addition to those set forth in this chapter.

4. Describe the last negotiation in which you participated and how you felt about both the process and the result.

5. Observe and report on a mediation process in your community.

6. Locate the *Labor Arbitration Reports* in your law library and review and report on a recent case.

7. Study the court system within your state. Diagram its structure and briefly describe the jurisdiction (authority) of each court.

8. Research what ADR programs are available to attorneys through the state bar association — e.g., fee disputes with clients, break-up of law partnerships, etc.

9. Determine if conflict or conflict management or dispute resolution is studied elsewhere on your campus or in local colleges or universities and what academic disciplines are offering the coursework or skills training and why.

Conflict

Introduction

Conflict is normal, healthy, and a positive force in everyone's life. It answers to many names and wears diverse faces. Examples include internal conflict that can occur within oneself over simultaneous job offers, within a family over financial matters, within an organization or a business over the breakup of that business, or within a political unit over environmental or spending issues. There is external conflict as well, which occurs between individuals, organizations (or between an individual and an organization), between and among political units, or within the natural environment. Think about examples of each of these. . . . More instances of conflict will come to mind.

Conflicts can be so small that they are hardly noticed or so large that they practically consume the participants, as well as anyone else touched by the conflict. An example of the latter is serious marital discord. Most conflicts fall somewhere between these two extremes. In our Western tradition, social interaction almost guarantees periodic conflict.

> [C]onflict plays a central role at all levels of our lives. At the intra personal level, we typically experience conflict each time we make a decision. Over time, these experiences are thought to serve as a foundation of our personalities and self-concepts. Conflict also shadows all of our interpersonal contacts, whether they involve work, play, or love. And as the scope of our interactions expands to include small and large groups, so too does the potential role of conflict expand.[1]

Conflict is a natural state that exists between people and groups, and no matter how hard social scientists try, they will never eliminate or totally resolve it.[2] For example, legal professionals face conflict on a continuing basis, not only through arguing on behalf of a client but by trying to persuade a client to appreciate a certain perspective. Conflicts also occur between attorneys, as well as staff members, within the same firm.

Conflict can be studied from a variety of perspectives. A sociologist will look at a conflict from a historical and social systems context. A political scientist will be interested in "political" conflicts and view them from a historical and political context. A psychologist will study conflict from the perspective of what feelings and emotions brought the parties to the conflict and how their dealing with the conflict will affect their future emotions and feelings. A feminist may see conflict as a power struggle between the sexes and a philosopher will view conflict from an ethical or theoretical point of view. Lawyers experience conflict in the form of lawsuits and disputes to be resolved within the legal system. There are people who study conflict and its resolution from a scientific, mathematical, and "game" theory perspective.

Similarly, individuals approach conflict from differing personal perspectives. Each person's point of view will depend on his or her emo-

---

1. Conflict Between People & Groups 1 (Stephen Worchel & Jeffrey A. Simpson eds., 1993) (citations omitted).
2. *Id.* at 76.

tional and psychological "baggage," life experience and perspective, and educational and cultural background. People are complex, and each disputing party, whether it is an individual or an organization, is complex. Some professionals, such as lawyers, are more comfortable working with conflict, particularly within the context of their profession. Other professional people may be less comfortable with conflict because they are conditioned to avoid or circumvent it.

An in-depth study of conflict will be left to the diverse theorists mentioned above and to others — anthropologists, businesspeople, and clinicians. It is necessary, however, for the student of dispute resolution to expand his or her understanding of conflict and its effect before proceeding to study its resolution. Part of the resolution process is to understand the conflict, its sources, the underlying interests, and the potential for management or resolution.

There is an urgency to the investigation of this topic that results from the "growing presence of conflict in the world. While modern advances in sciences have increased our options for travel, lengthened the days of our lives, and given us more leisure time than ever before, each of these gains has also provided greater opportunities for conflict to emerge at all levels of our lives."[3] This urgency has spilled over into the legal system, which is expanding the use of dispute resolution to meet the need of increased conflict, both within and outside of the courts.

What Is Conflict and How Is It Perceived?

According to one source, a conflict is "a prolonged battle; a struggle; clash; a controversy; disagreement; opposition."[4] Lawyers define a dispute as "a conflict or controversy; a conflict of claims or rights; an assertion of a right, claim or demand on one side, met by contrary claims or allegations on the other."[5] Most people can define conflict, and, more to the point, can think of innumerable examples. Another source states that "conflicts are more than just debates or negotiations. They represent

3. *Id.* at 2.
4. American Heritage Dictionary of The English Language, New College Edition (1979).
5. Black's Law Dictionary (6th ed. 1990).

17

an escalation of everyday competition and discussion into an arena of hostile or emotion-provoking encounters that strain personal or interpersonal tranquility, or both."[6]

To many people, conflict has a purely negative connotation. It is considered bad, distasteful, unpleasant, and, to some, it ranks up there right next to "sin." It is certainly true that conflict has the "enormous potential to destroy everything with which it comes in contact."[7] It has led to "war and the buildup of frightening arsenals of weapons. Conflict over values, goals, opportunities, and materials has split apart or destroyed groups."[8]

> Conflict and its most extreme disguise, competition, have been identified as the cause of intergroup hostility, prejudice, and discrimination. The roots of war are often deeply embedded in conflict over territory or basic attitudes and values.[9]

If understood correctly, however, conflict can bear positive fruit. It is an integral and necessary part of life and can be used creatively as a source of clarification, understanding, growth, learning, and communication.

> Conflict plays a positive role at all levels of human interaction (intrapersonal, interpersonal and intergroup). . . . [C]onflict causes the individual to go through a self-examination process. It motivates the individual to mobilize his or her capabilities to deal with or overcome the conflict. Through these efforts the individual becomes better able to define her or his abilities and self-concept.[10]

Conflict is meaningful and, in reality, is a normal response to an issue that is worth struggling over.[11]

> [C]onflict may [also] initiate broad and important social change. Looking within the United States, open and sometimes violent conflict between blacks and whites served as the stepping stone for reform of nearly every facet of life including education, voting, political districting, employment, law, and even the content of textbooks and popular television programming. Similar reforms can be attributed to conflict between people of different genders, religions, ages, and sexual orientations. It is a matter

---

6. Gini Graham Scott, Resolving Conflict 1 (1990).
7. Conflict Between People & Groups, *supra* note 1, at 2.
8. *Id.* at 82.
9. *Id.* at 79 (citations omitted).
10. Stephen Worchel et al., Toward a More Balanced View of Conflict: There is a Positive Side, *in* Conflict Between People & Groups, *supra* note 1, at 78.
11. Forum, National Institute for Dispute Resolution 11.3 (1994).

of speculation whether these changes would have occurred without open confrontation.[12]

The legal system and the professionals who work within it are frequently at the forefront of such changes.

Conflict cannot be ignored. It "demands attention, whether that attention be aimed at removing conflict, resolving it, managing it, or converting it from an evil force into a constructive one."[13] An increase in violence has gained the public's attention, and some see the integration of conflict resolution skills into public education as one response to that violence. An example is the development of the peer mediation movement in public schools. In peer mediation, students who have received conflict resolution training and training in mediation skills help other students who are in conflict work through their disputes.

One problem people generally encounter when they face up to the conflict in their lives is that their initial reaction is one of fear. People find themselves overwhelmed and afraid of their powerful and sometimes irrational feelings.

> The difficulty in dealing with conflict is that it touches a part of us that is not purely rational. We each have an emotional and affective side. In conflict this part is roused from its socialized slumber and we feel agitation, anger, even rage. . . . [A] great deal of the powerful energy in conflict arises from the feelings generated, rather than from the purely rational differences involved.[14]

Another problem with conflict is that "adults don't seem to know how to enter into (conflict) with integrity and respect and with some degree of confidence and hope."[15] As a result, many individuals spend a great deal of time and energy either avoiding conflict or avoiding an open discussion of it. "Conflict is the source of all growth and an absolute necessity if one is to be alive. . . . However, unfortunately for too many of us, the idea of conflict is a negative one because we lack the skills to manage disagreements in a healthy, peaceable and respectful way."[16]

> Conflict, intrapersonal, interpersonal, or intergroup, may be uncomfortable, stressful, and followed by destructive consequences. Conflict, itself,

12. Worchel et al., *supra* note 10, at 79-80.
13. Conflict Between People & Groups, *supra* note 1, at 2.
14. C. James Maselko, The Fair Fight (Effective Aggression) (Designed Learning Inc., Plainfield, N.J., 1985), at 1.
15. Selma Myers & Barbara Filner, Mediation Across Cultures: A Handbook about Conflict & Culture 10 (1993).
16. *Id.* at 12.

is not the smoke that signals that something is amiss within an individual or between individuals. Nor does conflict always require an immediate remedy to reduce its level. Rather, conflict is a natural and necessary part of life and social interaction. It is as likely to initiate deep and positive personal reflection as it is to result in personal distress. It is as likely to motivate growth in a relationship as it is to be a sign of a troubled relationship. And it is as likely to propel group development as it is to instigate intergroup destruction and prejudice.[17]

If conflict plays a role in creativity, conflict resolution, in turn, often demands a creative approach, requiring disputants to look beyond their usual mode of response to conflict and to develop new behaviors to achieve a lasting resolution.

> [F]requent conflict . . . can be the sign of a troubled relationship. [However,] numerous investigators have shown that a relationship without conflict, or one in which conflict is avoided, can be equally troubled. . . . Thus, far from being a destroyer, a certain degree of conflict can actually invigorate relationships. In any case, it is not the conflict that is the problem but rather the management and response to conflict that determines the health of the unit. . . . In addition to giving new energy to tired relationships, conflict can serve as a "warning signal" that a relationship is headed for serious problems and identify the nature of the problems.[18]

A reflection of this philosophy is the approach now common among divorce lawyers, who encourage new clients to seek marital counseling before deciding to pursue a divorce.

One must examine the sources of conflict and the bases for them. "Most times it is frustrating because we skip the step of identifying differences and immediately attempt resolution — without knowing what it is we are trying to resolve."[19] One writer theorizes about marital disputes that

> couples should not be too quick to jump into a conflict-resolving mode of behavior. Rather, their first response should be to analyze the conflict and determine the statement it is making about the relationship. . . . Couples are too ready to believe that their fight involves incompatible goals rather than a difference over the means of achieving a common goal.[20]

---

17. Worchel et al., *supra* note 10, at 88. For an in-depth look at the role of conflict in "group identity and group development," see *id.* at 82-86.

18. *Id.* at 78-79.

19. C. James Maselko, Support/Confrontation (Bock, Petrella, Weisbord, Plainfield, New Jersey, 1980), at 5.

20. Worchel et al., *supra* note 10, at 79.

In addition to studying the conflict, it is important to look at the stage the conflict has reached. Timing may be a critical issue in determining the value of conflict[21] and whether it is an appropriate time to attempt resolution. One must look at whether conflict is serving as a constructive process or as a destructive process. One must guard against "premature resolutions that obscure different interests and perspectives."[22]

Recent theory suggests that since not all conflict is "resolvable," we must learn to "manage" conflict.

> With proper conflict management skills, potential conflicts can be averted or defused — and even turned into a positive source for improved interpersonal relationships and personal growth. The key is not to avoid conflict, which is potentially inherent in all social interaction and in all personal choices we make, but to recognize it and manage it skillfully to produce the best outcome.[23]

Sources of Conflict

There are innumerable sources of conflict, which include miscommunication, differences, anger and mistrust, fear, misunderstanding or misperception, thwarted expectations and changing roles, limited resources, and "difficult people."[24]

Miscommunication

Failure of communication, incomplete communication, or incorrect communication are significant sources of conflict. If a communication is not understood, or only conveys part of the necessary information, or requires assumptions to be made by the listener, or is not made at all, conflict is a highly probable result. For example, if a teenager forgets to tell his parents that after the football game there is a party that he intends to attend and then arrives home very late, causing his parents to worry about safety, his failure to communicate is at least one of the

---

21. Conflict Between People & Groups, *supra* note 1, at 89.
22. Forum, National Institute for Dispute Resolution (1994), at 5.
23. Scott, *supra* note 6, at 2.
24. See also Infra, page 29.

sources of the ensuing conflict. If his parents then fail to effectively communicate to him that their anger arises from their concern for him, he may assume or believe that they just do not want him to grow up, or be independent, or have fun. If the teenager then storms out of the house in anger, the parents may assume he is being rebellious, when he is just venting his anger and giving himself time to cool down. And on . . . and on . . . and on. Similar miscommunications occur on all levels of personal interaction.

> Communication, the key to resolving most conflicts, is itself often the cause of conflict. Any breakdown of communication can lead to conflict; and there are numerous examples in everyday interactions. Sometimes one person isn't clear. Sometimes someone isn't listening. There are often misunderstandings about meanings. Hidden assumption can stand in the way. And sometimes there is no communication at all, resulting in misunderstandings, hostility, or resentment.[25]

One must bear in mind that communication is nonverbal as well as verbal. An individual may say one thing, but convey something else through nonverbal communication.

> Experts in the communication field tell us that we get about 55 percent of our information from the non-verbal communication that accompanies a spoken message (such as facial gestures and body movements). We get about 38 percent from the voice, pitch, tone, and sounds we hear; and only 7 percent from content. This means that we're remarkably likely to misinterpret or discredit the very message someone thinks he or she is communicating.[26]

Consider a co-worker who says "good morning" with a frown on his face. Isn't this likely to cause confusion, incorrect assumptions, or anger in the listener?

Simply and concisely put, the best way to deal with miscommunication, or lack of communication is to *communicate,* discuss what is unclear, make sure all participants understand each other, and listen effectively.

25. Scott, *supra* note 6, at 90.
26. *Id.* at 100.

Differences

The differences between individuals, organizations, and nations are a common source of conflict. Indeed, conflict may be inevitable because of our differences. Each person is different from others, each family is different, each community is different, each organization is different, each society is different, and each nation is different. While differences can be enriching, they can also cause alienation, isolation, and conflict. What are some of our differences?

[A]ge, sex, race, ethnicity, language, education, social status, economic status, geographic community, verbal and non-verbal expressions, hierarchy, manners, religion and spirituality, symbols, social control mechanisms, conformity/individuality, conceptions of the "self," expressions of emotions, fatalism/self-determinism, the role of sexual orientation, beliefs about fairness, honesty, and truth, conceptions of time, face-saving, uses of ritual and of course, beliefs about conflict.[27]

These are but representative examples. The general point is that sometimes, when we are in conflict, we are "simply making explicit the differences that exist between us."[28]

Some of the differences that have been mentioned can be characterized as cultural. That raises the question as to what constitutes "culture."

A narrow concept of "culture" includes what most of us think of immediately: elements such as nationality, ethnicity, language, religion. But while researchers do not agree on one definition of culture, there is a general consensus that a broad definition of culture is needed that takes into account demographic variables, status variables, and affiliation variables.[29]

Cultural differences, then, go far beyond race, religion, nationality, or gender.

[L]imiting consideration to objective culture (visible culture that can be identified from inside or outside of the group, such as language or nationality) without consideration of subjective culture (internalized attitudes, assumptions, opinions, and feelings held by group members) can

---

27. Judith A. Kruger & Michelle LeBaron Duryea, The Tapestry of Culture: A Design for the Assessment of Intercultural Disputes, *in* Taking Stock, 1992 Proceedings of 20th Annual Conference of Society of Professionals in Dispute Resolution (Oct. 1992), at 68.

28. Maselko, *supra* note 21, at 4.

29. Kruger & Duryea, *supra* note 29, at 66.

dangerously create or reinforce stereotypes, and shut down what should be a permanent, fluid learning process.[30]

Again, cultural diversity refers to more than race, ethnicity, or gender. It includes age, lifestyles, sexual orientations, contrasting abilities and skills, and other factors that "influence peoples' beliefs, values, assumptions and, in turn, their communication styles."[31] "We would define culture more informally as a set of rules, written and unwritten, which instruct individuals on how to operate effectively with one another and with their environment. It not only defines ways to act, but also ways to react, and thus is a valuable tool."[32]

Members of different cultures vary even in the way they attempt to persuade others to their position.

> In some cultures it is acceptable to marshal forcefully, but truthfully, all the arguments for one's own side and to avoid giving gratuitous help to the other side. In other cultures it is acceptable to exaggerate or even to bend the truth here and there — but not too much. In still other cultures a really big whopper, if accomplished with flair and humor, is something to brag about and not to hide after the fact, especially if it is successful.[33]

The legal profession itself is a form of a "culture." Legal personnel use a unique language and understand the legal arena of courts, contests, and conflict in a way that laypersons do not. They often deal with people in conflict and under stress. As a result, lawyers are frequently disliked or misunderstood by the general public; they are stereotyped, giving rise to many "anti-lawyer" jokes.

Think about all the things that contribute to making you a unique individual and how they could be considered part of your "culture." Given all of these characteristics that define who you are, stereotyping might seem like a natural result. However, one must assiduously avoid stereotyping, which can itself lead to conflict. Further,

> [o]ne must be cautious in classifying every dispute as cultural. It may simply be a personality clash between two individuals who dislike each other, or for whom the chemistry does not work. Even in such apparently non-cultural situations, the conflict may be exacerbated by cultural behaviors. . . . More difficult to identify are conflicts which arise from basic non-cultural issues, which somehow become overlaid with cultural dif-

---

30. *Id.* at 67.
31. Myers & Filner, *supra* note 15, at 35.
32. *Id.* at 34.
33. Howard Raiffa, The Art and Science of Negotiation 47 (1982).

ferences originating from values, beliefs and attitudes. Because culture is so deeply ingrained, individuals make cultural assumptions and may not be aware their assumptions are being challenged. Variations from the norm are often misjudged to be deviations.[34]

Some examples of differences that can create or exacerbate conflict include differing confrontation styles, differing attitudes toward conflict itself, differing levels of respect for others, such as the aged, and differing values placed on assertiveness and individual rights. For example, in the dominant United States culture, individualism is valued and independence in decision-making is important. In other cultures, the group is considered more important than the individual, and the desire for harmony exceeds the desire for individual recognition. In some cultural environments, physical closeness and direct eye contact is the norm while in others it is considered offensive or disrespectful. Some groups place significant emphasis on the present and the future, while others hold the past in greater reverence.

Although individual and cultural differences are an important source of conflict and it is therefore essential to be aware of them, they should not be overemphasized. One must keep in mind the similarities shared by diverse cultures and the universal aspects of all humanity.

Anger, Mistrust, and Fear

Other sources of conflict are anger, mistrust, and fear, which occur in most relationships. Each of these emotions can build up over time, especially if not recognized and dealt with directly when it first appears. In a relationship,

> [t]here can be real hurts, imagined hurts, and new hurts on top of past hurts, which keep mounting up. . . . [E]ach person thinks the other is acting out of bad will, and sees each new action, no matter how innocent, as another attack. Mistrust can be real or imagined. Fears can be rational or irrational, but they can interfere with a relationship and cause conflict. Conflicts often arise when people have underlying needs or strong wants that aren't being met, such as a desire for security, perhaps independence, or belonging. Conflicts also grow out of fears that something valuable may be lost: a friendship, property, peace and quiet.[35]

34. Myers & Filner, *supra* note 15, at 15.
35. Scott, *supra* note 6, at 69.

Lawyers seem to be trained to mistrust people. It helps them professionally to require others to prove their assertions. It aids them in preparing a contract to do so as if parties' rights under the document were going to be litigated in the future. Such a posture of mistrust, however, while potentially beneficial in a courtroom, can misfire in an office or a social setting; the attribute so important to a lawyer's professional success may itself be a source of conflict. It is not surprising, given their training and the necessities of their professional pursuits, that lawyers have a reputation for being abrupt and mistrustful.

Issues of anger, mistrust, and fear are best dealt with by confronting the feelings, discussing the feelings, and deciding whether the parties want to continue the relationship or end it. Without confronting the anger or mistrust, and thereby giving the parties an opportunity to express their feelings and to dissipate them, the relationship will continue to be unsatisfactory. Fear needs to be dealt with more sensitively, by attempting to recognize the fear in oneself or others, understanding that fear, and helping to alleviate it.

How can we confront these emotional barriers to harmony? One source indicates that we need to learn how to support another person *and* confront him at the same time.

> Support is accepting as valid for the other person whatever s/he says, thinks, feels, believes irrespective of my agreement. To accept as valid how the other perceives reality even though I do not share that view. Support is always for the other. It allows the other to be heard and understood, not necessarily agreed with.[36]

Most people need to be heard more than they need to have someone agree with them. It is an affirmation of their reality.

Facing conflict can result in confrontation. Confrontation is risky, but failure to confront is also risky because nothing changes. The "skill of confrontation is the ability to make explicit the differences between us without negating your position as valid for you. It requires me to acknowledge your position and differentiate yours from mine. The skill allows the differences to be clarified and explored prior to any attempt at problem solving."[37] This skill, along with enhanced communication skills, is essential in dealing with many of the sources of conflict covered in this chapter.

---

36. Maselko, *supra* note 21, at 2.
37. *Id.* at 6.

Responsibility

Misunderstandings and misperceptions can result from miscommunication. They can also result from conflict over shared responsibility — someone taking on too much responsibility or too little responsibility.

> These extremes in taking or giving responsibility can produce conflict because of the reaction they produce in others. When one person fails to take responsibility, others can resent being left with the blame or the work; while when someone takes on too much responsibility for something, and perhaps too much of the credit, others can feel resentful or alienated.[38]
>
> In one common situation, a person takes on extra responsibility because he or she doesn't think the other person is taking on enough. The other person is often unaware of the need for that responsibility. That person might also have different priorities, or might not see what has to be done since it is being done by the first person. This is a frequent source of conflict between husband and wife.[39]

Picture a situation in which there are two paralegals in a department. One always seems to have the responsible jobs, while the other seldom seems to work very hard. The one who has the responsible jobs feels important, but overworked. The individual who does not appear to be working hard may be fearful of responsibility and may resent the other paralegal. This situation is bound to result in conflict. The parties need to explore the realities of the conflict and develop a working relationship that will be responsive to both of their needs, as well as to those of their employer. This requires effective communication and each party's being open about their feelings. Only then can they develop a plan to avoid the "responsibility trap" in the future.

Expectations and Roles

Thwarted expectations and the way roles change can best be explained in the marital context. Each spouse comes from a unique family and has certain expectations based upon his or her own family experience. But because both spouses are different from their parents and each marriage is therefore unique, it is practically impossible to duplicate a marriage that one saw (or believed they saw) as a child. To further com-

---

38. Scott, *supra* note 6, at 49.
39. *Id.* at 60.

plicate the issue of expectations, the roles of men and women in marriage are evolving. A man whose father "ruled the house" may feel emasculated when he does not wield the same authority or receive the same expression of respect that his father did. Likewise, a woman whose mother did not work outside of the home and was able to expend all her energy on homemaking may feel like society and her husband demand too much of her, expecting her to have a career and maintain a home at the same time. Imagine two lawyers who are married to one another, each accustomed to having people (clients) listen to them and take their advice. To extend such expectations to their respective spouses will cause immediate and long-term conflict.

Similar conflicts can occur in the workplace. People accuse assertive women of being too aggressive, or individuals may have difficulty working for someone from an ethnic group they thought to be undeserving of such authority. As an example, it is only in the last 20 years that women and minorities have established their presence in the legal profession. An older secretary who has always worked for an older white male may resent a new attorney who is younger, or female, or from a racial minority. Any shift of roles and expectations can cause conflict.

A person needs to be realistic about the expectations he has of himself as well as of others. Such realism will contribute greatly toward avoiding conflicts based on faulty or outdated or unrealistic expectations. Further, each party to a conflict must see the other as a unique individual or entity, and not relate to the other on the basis of the "role" he is assumed to perform. If this is done and communication is open, the parties can explore together the inaccurate assumptions that lead to conflict.

Resources

Limited resources is an obvious source of conflict. When there is "too little to go around," children, adults, communities, states, businesses, and countries will vie over the available resources. Such competition is a major source of business for attorneys. A significant dispute resolution skill is to enlarge the "pie" over which the disputants are competing. This, however, cannot always be done and conflicts ranging from arguments to wars results.

When resources are limited, the parties must attempt to "satisfy as best as possible each person's highest priorities or most important needs in return for getting concessions on lower priority items or needs . . . or . . . try to find new alternative positions that provide good payoffs for both."[40] Some conflicts arising from limited resources are not capable of being resolved in the traditional way and the parties must creatively devise a process for dealing with future conflicts.

Difficult People

Some people are just difficult! They can be hostile, naysayers, know-it-alls, etc. To make this issue more complex, each of us reacts differently to different kinds of difficult people, i.e., some people are more able than others to "push our buttons" through their behavior. Some people despise liars, others abhor really aggressive individuals, and still others cannot deal with indecisive people.

The problem is not identifying difficult people but dealing with them. It has been suggested that an individual (1) work through one's own emotional charges triggered by difficult people and (2) try to determine why they are being difficult.[41] The latter is accomplished through effective communication. "[M]ost people are difficult because they have certain underlying needs or interests that they meet by acting that way. . . . Thus, if you decide it's worth it to deal with people who are difficult, you might look for these underlying needs and think of how you can satisfy them."[42]

We must also learn not to take other people's behavior personally. "[A]nother person's negative or provoking behavior is often not directed specifically at you. The other person might have a problem; it has nothing to do with you, so why take it on?"[43] This may be the secret technique used by the paralegal who is able to work with an attorney no one else can stand because he is so difficult.

Summary

Conflict is a natural occurrence and an integral part of everyone's life. It can be internal or external, brief or ongoing, personal or group conflict. It is a powerful positive force contributing to change and growth, re-

40. *Id.* at 157.
41. *Id.* at 182.
42. *Id.* at 180.
43. *Id.* at 35.

quiring attention and a creative response. It is important to understand conflict and its source prior to attempting to resolve conflict. As a society, we need to develop conflict management skills as well as techniques for conflict resolution.

There are many sources of conflict. Miscommunication is one of the most significant. It is effectively remedied, however, through recognition of the miscommunication and by sharpening our communication and listening skills.

The differences between and among individuals, groups, and nations can lead to misunderstanding, apprehension, fear, and stereotyping. While one must be aware of the differences and how they contribute to conflict, one also must be careful to not stereotype or see cultural differences as the cause of every conflict.

In order to understand conflict, one must be able to recognize anger, mistrust, and fear in oneself as well as others. Then one needs to confront these feelings in oneself, or, if they emanate from someone else, discuss with them the feelings and be supportive. This supportive attitude is really communicating that one hears and understands the other, which can be done without necessarily agreeing with the other.

How much responsibility one takes on can also be a source of conflict. Some individuals accept too much responsibility and later resent it; others accept too little responsibility and are resented. The best way to deal with these issues is to recognize them and openly discuss them so that the responsibility can be shared in a manner acceptable to all involved.

Unmet expectations and changing roles frequently contribute to conflict. Expectations, realistic or otherwise, are usually not communicated and frustration and anger result when they are not met. Once again, one must engage in a critical look at one's expectations and role stereotypes and, if appropriate, share one's perspectives on these issues with the other person.

We all know someone who could be described as "difficult." And, politically, we may have definite ideas about which nations we have an uneasy alliance with. Frequently, individuals and nations are "difficult" because they have unmet needs. If one chooses to deal with them, or must deal with them, it is best to determine what those unmet needs are. In addition, in dealing with difficult people, one must be careful not to take their anger personally.

There is a three-step pattern here that deserves attention. In most conflict situations, one must ferret out and understand the source of the conflict, realistically analyze it, and communicate effectively about it. This three-step analysis should be directed to oneself as well as to one's relationship with others. Before we blame others for the conflict, we should first look at ourselves.

30

EXERCISES

1. Maintain a weekly conflict journal, in which you describe at least one personal conflict for each week and indicate what you believe the source of the conflict was, whether it was resolved, how it was resolved, and how you feel about the conflict and its resolution or nonresolution.

2. Choose one of the conflict sources covered in this chapter and create a law office scenario demonstrating how it works to create conflict.

3. Locate, read, and report on a scholarly article about conflict from another academic perspective, e.g., anthropology, sociology, math, psychology, history, or philosophy.

4. Describe how you feel when you are in conflict with someone and how you believe the other person feels. Describe how you feel when you observe others in conflict.

5. Find and report on a historic example of how conflict was productive and brought about positive change.

6. In an ongoing relationship, how would you manage the negative part of conflict and give the positive side an opportunity to expand?

7. Describe a conflict (yours or someone else's) in which you believe that the failure to effectively communicate was one of the sources of the conflict.

8. Describe two families (e.g., neighbors, in-laws, etc.) you have observed in a relationship with each other, and indicate how their respective family cultures differed. Overall, did these differences enrich the relationship or cause conflict, or both.

9. Read and report on a scholarly or business article describing how communication styles differ according to nation of origin; for example, differing communication styles between Japanese and American businesspeople.

10. Practice being supportive of another without necessarily agreeing with their point of view. Describe how you did this and the re-

sult. Do this several times and determine if this is an aid in conflict management and resolution.

11. Describe a situation in which you feel you took on too much responsibility. Describe another in which you assumed too little responsibility. How would you change these in the future.

12. List your expectations of this class; describe how the reality of the class differs from your expectations.

Negotiation

Introduction

Introduction

Negotiation is defined in several ways: "The deliberation, discussion, or conference upon the terms of a proposed agreement; the act of settling or arranging the terms and conditions of a bargain, sale, or other business transaction."[1] Or, to negotiate is "to hold communication or conference (with another) for the purpose of arranging some matter by mutual agreement; to discuss a matter, with a view to some settlement or compromise."[2] Some would say that negotiation is really the act of attempting to persuade others to adopt your point of view.

Everyone negotiates — friends, enemies, and strangers alike. Children negotiate amongst themselves over family responsibilities; com-

1. Black's Law Dictionary (6th ed. 1990).
2. 10 Oxford English Dictionary 303 (2d ed. 1989).

muters negotiate over who will drive to work; students negotiate study assignments; spouses negotiate with each other daily; consumers negotiate to purchase a car or a house; and employees and employers negotiate over salary and benefits. It is carried on face-to-face, over the telephone, in writing, and through third parties. Negotiation, in one form or another, is an integral part of our lives.

Is negotiation a skill that can be learned, a science that may be predicted, or an art practiced only by those people who have the gift? There are elements of all three in negotiation; but learning the skills and techniques, engaging in appropriate preparation, understanding the process, and, of course, practice all aid in the development of a more sophisticated and informed negotiating ability.

Negotiation Theories

Competitive Approach

There are a number of approaches to negotiation. One is the competitive, "all-for-me" approach. In the extreme, the negotiator is attempting to win as much as possible, regardless of the cost. If winning is the sole criterion, this type of negotiator is frequently successful, because a competitive negotiator can overpower and overwhelm an opponent. However, this approach may also result in failure because it inflames the other side or pushes so hard that no agreement is reached. Or an agreement may be reached, but subsequently not honored; an agreement that someone is badgered into accepting is less likely to be honored than one that is reached as a result of everyone's active participation. Another negative result of overtly competitive behavior is the reputation the negotiator develops, which may make future negotiations more difficult.

Cooperative Approach

A different approach to negotiation is the cooperative one, sometimes called the "win-win" approach of Fisher and Ury's *Getting to Yes.*[3] Negotiators are encouraged to attempt to get beyond positional bargaining ("This is what I want and that is that!") and determine the underlying interests of each party so that they can creatively fashion an

---

3. Roger Fisher et al., Getting To Yes (2d ed. 1991).

agreement that is more likely to meet all the parties' needs. One technique in cooperative negotiation, rather than dividing up an existing pie, the negotiators expand the pie. While such an approach cannot work in all situations — it would not be applicable, for example, where price is the only issue — the techniques and attitudes of the cooperative approach provide a more congenial environment for any type of negotiation.

The ultimate goal is to maximize everyone's opportunity for gain:

> Searching for joint gains should be distinguished from compromising, which requires that everyone give up something. The goal in collaborative negotiation is to find solutions that satisfy everyone's interests, not to leave everyone with less than was hoped. "Splitting the difference" in compromise merely distributes the pain of losing — and often rewards the more unreasonable bargainer to boot.[4]

DISTRIBUTIVE VS. INTEGRATIVE BARGAINING

Single-issue negotiation, in which it is not possible to expand the field of issues, requires distributive bargaining, i.e., "more for me is less for you." Multiple-issue negotiation calls for integrative bargaining, i.e., a trading of issues. Sometimes a single-issue problem can be enlarged to include additional issues.

> Frequently the parties to a negotiation can do better by elaborating the problem and converting a single-factor negotiating problem into a multiple-factor problem. Often the motivation to do so is the fact that without this type of elaboration no agreement can be reached, and the bargaining principals may feel uncomfortable about not reaching an agreement.[5]

LINKING ISSUES

A technique commonly used to create or enlarge the issues in a negotiation is linkage. Here, the parties agree to future relations, such as future working arrangements and/or contracts. An agreement to provide future contracts links the successful negotiation of current disputes to expanded business between the parties, thereby providing for tradeoffs.

---

4. Linda R. Singer, Settling Disputes: Conflict Resolution in Business, Families, and The Legal System 17 (2d ed. 1994).
5. Howard Raiffa, The Art & Science of Negotiation 102 (1982).

FLEXIBILITY

A good negotiator will be able to combine the strategies of the various negotiation styles and be flexible enough to determine the optimum use of each. In addition, a good negotiator will know herself, i.e., have a realistic understanding of her own abilities and the style with which she is most comfortable.[6] A negotiator is most effective when acting in a manner that is consistent with her personality and preferences regarding human interaction.

EXAMPLES

What are the differences between competitive and cooperative approaches in an actual negotiation? Assume an individual needs to purchase a used car for work and school. He has saved $1,000 and does not want to pay more than that because his job is too insecure to justify getting involved in monthly payments. A "friend-of-a-friend" is selling a five-year-old compact car with high mileage. She is asking $1,500 for it. The friend indicates that as far as he knows, the owner has had no accidents and no significant mechanical problems with the car. The buyer could approach the situation by telling the owner everything he thinks is wrong with the car and saying it is not worth more than $800. This reflects a competitive approach. Conversely, he could discuss what the "blue book" value is, what his needs are, and what he is able to afford, while trying to find out what the seller's needs are. Does she need the money from this car as a down payment on another car? Is she leaving the area, or for some reason no longer needs a car? For both parties to work together to meet both their needs reflects a cooperative approach.

Dealing only with the issue of price would be a distributive approach and might result in no bargain being struck. However, after talking with each other for some time, the parties might discover that the car owner is having computer problems in her business and the purchaser is a computer whiz. An exchange for value could be made wherein the purchaser would provide future computer troubleshooting services to the seller in exchange for a lowering in the price of the automobile now. This approach reflects the use of linkage and an integrative approach.

---

6. There is a computer program, called "Negotiator Pro," that helps one undertake the sort of self analysis that is helpful here. It is available from Beacon Expert Systems, Inc., 35 Gardner Road, Brookline, Ma.

One-Text Approach

A third approach to negotiation is called the one-text approach. Here, one party offers a single proposal dealing with all the issues between the disputants. Then, the next party modifies the proposal and passes it on to the next party (if there is one) for further modification, until all parties have had their input. This process continues until the disputants reach a consensus on the total package. The one-text approach has the benefit of focusing on the dispute and using a joint effort to reach a resolution, rather than focusing on the differences between the parties. This approach is especially beneficial in multi-party negotiations, which "are often too diffuse to be effective unless they focus on a single negotiating text."[7] Sometimes the text is proposed by an intervenor. For an example of such an approach, look at a discussion of the Camp David negotiations in Howard Raiffa's *The Art & Science of Negotiation*.[8]

Theory Summary

There are two basic approaches to bargaining: competitive and cooperative. The competitive approach has historically been favored by attorneys, who bargain very hard to get the most for their clients. Current theory, however, supports the cooperative approach in order for both parties to achieve the maximum joint gains. A negotiator should be sufficiently flexible to employ a combination of both to achieve the best outcome. Distributive versus integrative bargaining is a comparison of negotiation based upon the number of issues. In distributive bargaining, it is best to expand the issues so that integrative bargaining can occur. Linkage is a vehicle whereby the negotiation is linked to future dealings between the parties, thereby expanding the issues.

The one-text approach to bargaining occurs when all issues are joined in one solution and the solution is then modified until the parties find the total package acceptable.

7. Raiffa, *supra* note 5, at 254.
8. *Id.* at 205.

Preparation for Negotiation

Most productive activity requires preparation. Negotiation is no different. Clearly, the preparation necessary or possible will vary depending on the situation. However, preparedness, mixed with flexibility, benefits even the most skilled negotiator. How can one best prepare?

Factual Preparation

Obtain all the factual information possible about the product or conflict, the people, your position, the other side's position, the market, and your alternatives. For example, Hannah, a college student, is moving to the town in which her college is located and wants to rent a room or apartment off-campus. She has looked at two apartments advertised in the newspaper and she likes one of them but does not feel she can afford the rent of $500 per month. She will be meeting with the landlord soon to negotiate an agreement. How can she prepare for this meeting?

Hannah can investigate other rentals by contacting a local realtor, which will provide a better picture of the local market. She can compare this with on-campus housing by speaking with the college housing office. She can also speak with other students to gain their perspective. Then she can speak with tenants in the building in which she wishes to rent in order to gather information regarding the landlord and the apartment building. She might also ask to see a copy of the landlord's lease ahead of time so that she can review it at her own pace. Information about the security of the area can be learned by contacting the police.

In addition, Hannah may need to review her own budget and additional funding sources that are available. She must determine the highest amount she can afford to pay for rent. Can she get a job on campus or near the apartment? She should contact the financial aid office regarding those resources. Hannah must also project what the landlord's interests may be. How long has the apartment been vacant? Are there other apartments in the building that are vacant? Is the property maintained well? Consider whether the landlord might exchange services, such as lawn care and snow removal, for a percentage of the rent.[9]

---

9. For an excellent example of factual and tactical preparation for negotiation, flexibility during negotiation, and the results, see the description of the negotiation regarding Elmtree House in *id.* at 35-43.

Role-Playing

In addition to factual preparation, preparing for negotiation should also include role-playing. In such a simulation, two or more individuals will act out the negotiation, trying out various case scenarios and playing both sides of the conflict. This increases one's confidence and comfort level with the process, aids in strategizing, and permits experimentation with various negotiation styles.

Other Determinations

In addition to factual preparation, the party must determine who is the best negotiator — the party himself, an attorney, or some other representative. If the party is actually a group of people, such as a school or synagogue, should the negotiator be someone in the group with experience in negotiation, someone in the group with experience related to the subject matter of the dispute, or someone with past experience dealing with the other party.

Preparation includes the negotiator knowing himself, his needs, and his best alternative to a negotiated agreement (BATNA). It includes analyzing goals or aspiration levels and placing a value on them, searching for alternatives, setting the reservation price, and developing and organizing arguments. Goals or aspiration levels represent the optimum settlement for a party. Valuation of them has to do with "deciding what one wants . . . and what they would be willing to give up in order to achieve their goal. One approach is to try to generate scoring systems that assign points to various levels within each attribute and that quantify tradeoffs between issues."[10] Reservation price is the absolute minimum that a negotiating party will accept. When an agreement isn't reached even after resorting to one's reservation price, one should have an idea of a preferred BATNA, which is what one would want to happen when the disputants fail to settle.

Preparation also includes analyzing the other disputants, their potential goals, reservation price, BATNA, and negotiating style. Finally, one should be aware of the negotiating customs of the country or region and of the parties. For example, is lying an acceptable behavior in this type of negotiation?

---

10. *Id.* at 148.

Time, Place, and Parties

Prior to the actual meeting, the parties should set a time and place for the negotiation. The time should be mutually agreed upon and location can be at a neutral site or at one of the party's place of business. Who should participate in the negotiation is a more complex issue. While the identity of the parties in a two–party dispute may be clear, they may want to bring a family member or community elder to the mediation. To exclude them might have a negative impact on the disputant's ability to effectively participate in the negotiation; to permit a nonparty to be present, however, may alter the power balance. In a dispute over an environmental issue, on the other hand, even identifying all the parties in question is not so easy. Questions arise as to what special interest groups should be involved and who will protect the interests of the public. Sometimes the field of potential parties is too broad; the issue as to who attends the negotiation may therefore become one of the issues to be negotiated.

Flexibility

As already mentioned, in addition to preparation, it is important to remain flexible. Flexibility requires the negotiator to periodically reassess her interests and positions and the projected interests and positions of the other party based upon information acquired during negotiation. Flexibility also requires the negotiator to remain open to new ideas and suggestions that may come from the other side. It is helpful to view the negotiation as an opportunity for an exchange of ideas and options looking toward joint gains, rather than a struggle to obtain one's own desired outcome.

Essential Steps in the Process

After thorough preparation, establishing the meeting place, and determining who will participate, the actual negotiating meeting takes place. While negotiations can and do take place over the telephone, a face-to-face meeting allows the parties to observe each other during negotiation, encourages total concentration without distraction, and demonstrates a commitment to the process. At the meeting, some negotiators will want to get the easy issues out of the way first and get the parties in an "agreeing" frame of mind. Others may want to tackle the most difficult areas first. Some negotiators will establish an agenda of the issues to be covered, while others want to leave the structure more free-flowing. In this respect, there is no right or wrong way. It will depend on the negotiators, the parties, and the conflict.

Preliminary Negotiations

"Opening gambits" — the first steps taken in the negotiation process — involve finding out more about the other side's positions, confirming facts, introducing outside standards, and perhaps making initial offers. Some negotiators are more willing to provide factual information than others. Obtaining as much factual information as possible is essential to an informed negotiation and settlement. The use of outside standards (e.g., using an independent appraisal of real estate to establish value or using the "blue book" value for automobiles) has a neutralizing effect. Each negotiator should try to explore the other party's underlying interests and cautiously convey her own. Opening offers should be neither too extreme nor too conservative.

Central Negotiations

The next step of formal negotiations has been called the "negotiation dance." Once negotiations begin in earnest, it is important to be aware of concessions, how frequently they are made, and how much is conceded in each. The rate of concessions may increase as parties near an agreement. There may be some trading of issues: one party may feel intractable on one issue, but is willing to concede on another. These must be explored. Concessions made by one side are usually linked to the other party's concessions. If an impasse is reached on one issue, move on to the next and return to the impasse later.

Brainstorming can be helpful in this stage. It allows the parties to offer suggestions without being committed to them. "Negotiations are most productive when parties feel comfortable inventing solutions without committing to them — at least not until all possible outcomes have been identified and evaluated."[11] Issue clarification by each party is important at this stage.

Here again the importance of flexibility must be stressed. A negotiator must be ready to reevaluate her goals, reservation price and BATNA throughout the negotiations, based upon altered perceptions

11. Singer, *supra* note 4, at 18.

and acquisition of new information. For example, if one goes into an employment negotiation with a particular understanding of the job description and determines during the negotiation that the job description is different than initially believed, such information could alter goals, reservation price (or salary), and BATNA. If, during the course of a negotiation over the rental of an apartment, the landlord learns that the tenant, who is a second-year graduate student, also has a permanent teaching position at the university, the landlord may alter his perception of the longevity of the leasehold, which can affect other issues being discussed.

Timing is also very important. A good negotiator is patient and sensitive to the other party's sense of time.

> [T]he bargainer who is willing to wait longer, to probe more patiently, to appear less eager for a settlement will be more successful. . . . Many Americans are uncomfortable with long pauses in the give-and-take of negotiations. They feel obliged to say something, anything, to get the negotiations rolling. However, it's not what is said in negotiations that counts, but what isn't said. Very often the strategic essence of a negotiation exercise is merely a waiting game with self-imposed penalties (embarrassment) for delays.[12]

Closing of Negotiations

At the end of the negotiation, parties should be in a position to make commitments. If total agreement cannot be reached in one session, affirm those issues that have been agreed upon and establish another meeting date and time. If all issues are resolved, confirm the resolution in writing, if appropriate, review them to make sure all parties understand and are satisfied, confirm that there are no other outstanding issues, and end the meeting. If no agreement can be reached, end the meeting, but leave the door open for future negotiations. Such future negotiations might include introducing an intervenor or broadening the issues being negotiated.

Other Factors

These steps in the process of negotiation will be affected by the number and complexity of issues, the number of parties involved, whether the parties are present, whether there are party representatives,

---

12. Raiffa, *supra* note 5, at 78.

the experience the negotiators and/or the parties have with each other, the custom of the area (both geographical and professional) and the culture of the parties.

Complex issues, numerous issues, and/or numerous parties will generally require more than one negotiation session. However, "[b]ecause of the possibilities for trade-offs, multi-issue disputes often turn out to be easier to resolve than single issues, which may allow less room for creative swaps."[13] As for multi-party disputes, "there is [also] a vast difference between conflicts involving two disputants and those involving more than two disputants. Once three or more conflicting parties are involved, coalitions of disputants may form and may act in concert against the other disputants."[14] To put it differently, "[i]f you decide not to come to an agreement with all of your adversaries, you might still forge an agreement with a subset of the other parties. In other words, you can still cooperate with a coalition of some of the others. If there is only one other party, this complexity can't be formulated."[15]

Representatives of a party who is not present at the negotiation, such as attorneys, may need to confirm any agreement with their client. When a party comprises a group of people, there may be conflict within that group as to the desired outcome and a negotiator will have to deal with those conflicts.

If the parties or their representatives are accustomed to dealing with each other, such as in labor negotiations, there will be certain customs and relationships that have built up over the years that will affect negotiations. Finally, the custom of the business or profession — e.g., realtors, car dealers, builders, landlords — as well as the custom of the area — e.g., northeast vs. southwest, American vs. Japanese — will affect the formalities and structure of the process.

Other peripherals that can affect negotiating include "differences in initial endowments or wealth, differences in time-related costs, differences in perceived determination or aggressiveness, differences in marginal valuations, differences in needs, and differences in the number of people comprising each side."[16]

Enforceability of a negotiated agreement can be an issue. We generally consider a negotiated agreement a contract, which is enforceable in a civil suit. Sometimes, such a settlement is made part of a court judgment and enforceable as such.

However, consider an international agreement, in which there is no enforcement mechanism. Scholars of this subject have determined

13. Singer, *supra* note 4, at 8.
14. Raiffa, *supra* note 5, at 11.
15. *Id.* at 252.
16. *Id.* at 54.

that "[t]he best way to secure a contract, when there are no binding, legal, enforcement mechanisms, is through the linkages of continuing involvement."[17] For example, consider a major power that wants to set up oil drilling in a small country but is concerned that once the drilling is established, the small country will force it to leave and will take over the operation. What authority could the major country go to for enforcement of the original agreement? In this case, the major power could allay its concerns by linking the successful operation of the drilling sites to continuing preferred trading status to the minor nation. Such status would be too beneficial to the smaller nation to jeopardize by taking over the drilling sites. Obviously, linkages can be made in domestic situations as well.

Summary

Negotiation takes place in stages and each stage contains several steps. There are three basic stages to each negotiation: preliminary discussions, the central part of the negotiation, and the closing. Negotiations are affected by the number of parties and issues, the presence of representatives, differing cultures, and the enforceability of the contract, among others. In preparing for or studying a negotiation, one should consider the following:

1. How many parties are involved?
2. If a party consists of a group, are they united in their goals?
3. Will these parties or these negotiators face each other again in the future?
4. Can the current issues be linked to future contacts?
5. How many issues are there?
6. Is an agreement required by law, as for public employees?
7. Are the parties to the dispute present at the negotiating table, or is ratification required?
8. Should a competitive or cooperative approach be utilized?
9. Are there time constraints or time-related costs?
10. Are the contracts binding?
11. Are the negotiations private or public?
12. What are the group norms: cooperative? competitive? in-between?
13. Is third-party intervention possible or appropriate?[18]

17. *Id.* at 198. See also discussion of examples at 196-197.
18. *Id.* at 11-19.

Communication Skills

Verbal Communication

The most important communication skill in the negotiation process is the ability to express an idea or concept in a nonthreatening and nonjudgmental way. For example, in negotiating the purchase of a car, the skilled buyer might say, "I hear you saying that you believe the car is actually worth $1,200. I don't agree with you; but let's look at the 'blue book' value or at advertisements for similar cars in the newspaper. It's not that I undervalue your car, I can really only afford to pay $800." A more confrontational buyer, on the other hand, might say, "That car isn't worth $500.00, much less $1,200! How stupid can you be? (or do you think I am?) I wouldn't pay more than _____ for that piece of junk!" The person selling the car is much more likely to respond positively to the first communication rather than the second. Why? It focuses on the issue at hand, not the people, and it utilizes outside standards or criteria as a basis for setting value.

How can this expressive ability be developed? One way is to practice. Part of cooperative communication is to address the issue, not attack the other person. One can honestly disagree as to the value of a car, but calling the other person names or disparaging her property or her position accomplishes little. One way to practice this skill is to speak with someone with whom you disagree on a particular issue. See if you can express your point of view in a nonthreatening and respectful manner. After the other side also expresses her ideas, reword her position as a way of communicating that you understand that position. This latter skill reflects the second most important communication skill — active listening and the ability to reword and repeat what someone else has said.

Listening Skills

Active, concentrated listening is essential. A person cannot effectively listen if her mind is elsewhere, thinking, for example, about what she is going to say when the speaker is finished talking. Neither can someone read this text and understand it while worrying about whether he will do well on the examination in this course. An individual must concentrate on the matter at hand: She must listen, take time to reflect, and then either respond or rephrase what she hears the other person has said. This approach has two benefits, it helps the listener understand the other person's position better and it conveys to the speaker that you have been listening to them. Think about how frustrating it is to speak to someone who is not listening to you!

The following checklists can serve as guidelines for improving listening skills.

Active Listening Skills

1. Maintain eye contact.
2. Make appropriate verbal responses to what the speaker says.
3. Pay attention. Don't let your mind wander to something else or to what you are going to say when the other person stops talking.
4. Maintain attentive body language.
5. Stop doing other things.
6. Avoid distractions, i.e., TV, radio, others talking.
7. Listen for feelings.
8. Encourage "I" messages.

Reflective Listening Skills

1. Restate what the other person has said, and obtain their affirmation that your understanding is accurate.
2. Restate what the other person has said in nonjudgmental language.
3. Ask the speaker to clarify what they have said.
4. Keep your demeanor and tone of voice calm.
5. Appear interested.
6. Summarize what the person has said.

Nonverbal Communication

Communication is more than just the use of words. It comprises all the ways in which someone has an impact on another person. Nonverbal communication includes the volume, rate, and pitch of one's voice, as well as body language and facial expressions. For example, while we might like to believe that our pets understand the words we use, it is more likely that they respond to the manner in which we say things. Try saying to a dog in an authoritative manner, "Tasha, go lay down." Then say "Tasha, go eat your dinner" in the same tone of voice, with the same inflection. She will probably react in the same way; that is, she will respond as if she is being disciplined. Repeat both statements in a loving, kind, and encouraging voice and she will respond to those statements as if she were being praised. Similarly, a person's response to some communication is influenced, and sometimes determined, by the manner in which it is communicated.

Other Issues

People react or respond differently to a speaker who speaks loudly, with medium volume, or quietly. Someone who has some difficulty hearing may prefer a loud speaker. A quiet person may prefer a quiet speaker. A speaker should control the volume of his speech so that others can comfortably hear without being overly loud. The rate of one's speech also bears attention. If a listener herself is a rapid speaker and is listening to a slower speaker, she might be tempted to finish sentences for the slower speaker. This can be very annoying and can result in miscommunication. Respect for other people's pace is an integral part of good communication. A speaker must also be aware of the pitch (high, medium, or low) of his voice and its impact on others.

The speaker needs to be sensitive to these things in himself and in others to be an effective communicator. A good negotiator is aware of the spoken language he uses as well as the power of his nonverbal communication. He is also aware of these in others and his reaction to them. Have you ever wondered why some people really "get on your nerves," even though they have said or done nothing to justify your annoyance? Perhaps the manner in which they communicate reminds you of someone you dislike. In negotiating with such a person, you would have to be aware of your reaction and guard against its influencing your ability to effectively communicate and negotiate.

Applications

Professional Fulfillment

While the skills involved in negotiation have broad life applications, the purpose here is to focus on paralegal applications. First is the area of professional self-improvement. As a paralegal, one negotiates for promotions, raises, benefits, particular work assignments, continuing education, and professional opportunities.

Consider the following situation: A paralegal, who has worked in a medium-sized law firm for approximately two years, wants to attend continuing education seminars periodically and wants the firm to pay for these seminars and give him time off to attend them. First the preparation: He should determine what the firm policy has been previously with regard to continuing education opportunities, for attorneys as well as paralegals; determine how other similarly sized firms treat the issue; approximate the cost to the firm in dollars and lost time; and approximate the benefit to the firm in expanded knowledge and improved morale. He should consider approaching others in the firm regarding who in authority should be asked about this issue and how they should be approached.

Next, the paralegal must practice the negotiation several times with a friend and then make an appointment with the individual in the firm who makes these personnel decisions. When commencing the negotiation, he will present his best position and try to obtain from the other person their underlying interests. How can both parties have their needs met within the framework of the firm and its resources? He should ask the other person what she suggests be done to resolve the issue. Encourage brainstorming. Remember, it is the problem that must be solved, not the parties who should be attacked. The paralegal must demonstrate to the manager or partner that he is sensitive to her issues as well as his own, but is firm in attempting to satisfying his needs. If the attorney or manager reacts in an unpleasant way, he should leave the door open for future negotiations. If a resolution cannot be reached, he will try to make sure there is an opportunity for further discussions.

Advocacy

Taking these skills a step further, when can paralegals apply their ability to negotiate in their role as a paralegal? In most states, they cannot negotiate on behalf of a firm's client regarding settlement of a matter or the terms of a contract. However, as an advocate in situations where they are permitted to represent clients, paralegals will negotiate on behalf of the client. Paralegals in legal services or paralegal advocates in public interest law firms can, with attorney supervision, represent disenfranchised clients before state and federal administrative agencies or judges. They may negotiate with the Social Security Administration regarding an overpayment of social security benefits where the Administration is seeking reimbursement. Legal Services clients may need the paralegal to negotiate on their behalf with a utility company to develop a payment plan for unpaid utility bills in order to avoid the cessation of services. On the state level, a paralegal may negotiate with welfare agencies regarding benefits for a client or appear before an administrative agency on the client's behalf. A paralegal working for the Office of Housing and Urban Development or a similar agency on the state level may negotiate with a landlord on behalf of an individual receiving a subsidy to work out a plan for correction of housing violations so that the rent subsidy can continue.

On Behalf of the Employer

Another negotiating opportunity exists for a paralegal in dealing with vendors of products and services for the firm. For example, a paralegal may be asked to determine which litigation software is best suited for the firm or corporate legal department and then negotiate with the vendor regarding installation, training, and support. An office manager may engage the services of a temporary personnel agency and negotiate the terms of the relationship on behalf of the employer.

Assisting the Attorney

A paralegal may be asked to prepare a client and/or the client's file for a negotiation session. This entails factual research and legal research, as well as educating the client as to what to anticipate. Perhaps the attorney will ask the paralegal to play the adversary role in a mock negotiation with the attorney.

A paralegal should observe as many negotiations as possible and, with the theoretical and skill-based knowledge acquired here, analyze each negotiation. Perhaps the attorney would appreciate feedback from the paralegal after the negotiation and ask the paralegal to participate in an analysis of the negotiation. Perhaps the paralegal can serve as a consultant during breaks in the negotiation. If the paralegal has substantive knowledge in a particular area which the attorney lacks, she can be an indispensable advisor in a negotiation.

Paralegals frequently have extensive client contact. Their ability to be good listeners and effective communicators enhances their relationship with the client and their ability to gather information, resulting in their increased value to the law firm. Good communication skills should also contribute to a "kinder" work environment.

Finally, the paralegal should be familiar with the attorney's obligation to pursue settlement on behalf of the client. Several federal rules[19]

19. Fed. R. Civ. P. 16 and 68.

require settlement offers to be made and responded to in an attempt to encourage serious negotiations to settle litigation, with the potential for sanctions for failure to comply. Many states have similar provisions in their court rules or statutes. Likewise, the National Labor Relations Act requires the parties to bargain in good faith.

Rulemaking Negotiation

Many people think of negotiating in terms of resolving an existing conflict. However, negotiation and mediation are becoming tools for developing legislation and making rules for broad promulgation. A paralegal working with a legislator or an agency (state or federal) that develops and proposes legislation and/or rules may be involved in such rulemaking negotiation with parties who have conflicting interests in the proposed legislation or rules.[20] This process is called "negotiated rulemaking" or "reg-neg."

Ethics

Ethical Rules

Attorney negotiators are bound by the American Bar Association's Rules of Professional Conduct[21] as adopted by the state in which they practice. These rules require honesty, professionalism, and fair dealing. Paralegals who work with attorneys are agents of the attorneys and must comply with the same rules.[22] In addition, both the National Federation of Paralegal Associations (NFPA) and the National Association of Legal Assistants (NALA) have promulgated rules regarding the behavior of paralegals. The American Arbitration Association, the American Bar Association, and the Society of Professionals in Dispute Resolution developed Model Standards of Conduct for Mediators (see Appendix A).

Attorneys have no affirmative duty to inform others of relevant facts. It is the responsibility of both sides to do their own research, factual investigation, and discovery. An attorney cannot expect his adversary to do his work for him.

---

20. Singer, *supra* note 4, at 24.
21. Model Rules of Professional Conduct 4.1(a), 4.2(a) (1983, 1995 ed.).
22. NALA Canon 12.

Representative Conflict

A concern for attorney or other agent negotiators is the potential conflict between their own personal and professional interests and those of the client in negotiating a settlement. In avoiding litigation by negotiating a settlement that is satisfactory to the client, the attorney is potentially reducing her own fee, whether it is on an hourly basis or is a contingency fee. Of primary importance is the rule that all settlement offers must be communicated to the client and the client must ultimately decide whether or not to accept the offer (Model Rules of Professional Conduct 1.2(a), 4). Such a decision is often made with the advice of counsel; but just as litigation is authorized by the client, so is the settlement. In providing advice to the client, the attorney must be aware of her own self-interests and not let those interests interfere with the client's decision.

Other potential scenarios of conflict include an attorney who is intent on searching for an objectively fair and impartial outcome and a client who simply wants the best possible outcome for himself. Or consider the potential conflict between a client who, because of a valuable long-term relationship, wants to maintain good relations with the other side, but is represented by someone who is out to get the most for his client and thereby enhance his reputation as a "killer."[23]

"Differing goals and standards of agent and principal may create conflicting pulls. For example, the buyer's agent may be compensated as a percentage of the purchase price, thus creating an incentive to have the price as high as possible. The buyer, of course, wants the lowest possible price."[24]

Truth

One walks a fine line between negotiating aggressively on behalf of oneself or another and not misrepresenting or lying about the issues. Exaggeration or "puffing" is permitted, but factual misrepresentation is not. In negotiating the sale and purchase of an automobile, for example, the parties can exaggerate or understate what they believe the value of the car to be; but neither party should misrepresent such matters as whether the car has been involved in an accident or one's ability to pay. Consider the case in which the seller of an auto represented to the pur-

23. Stephen B. Goldberg et al., Dispute Resolution: Negotiation, Mediation, and Other Processes 72 (1992).
24. *Id.* at 72.

chaser that he was selling it for a friend and that it had not been in an accident. The purchaser bought the car and subsequently found out that the seller was selling it for a dealership and that it had been in an accident and the frame had been damaged. The seller was guilty of fraud in this case.

The role that truth plays in negotiation will depend on the parties, the environment, and the issues. A certain degree of exaggeration is acceptable in some situations and frowned upon in others.

> The art of compromise centers on the willingness to give up something in order to get something else in return. Successful artists get more than they give up. A common ploy is to exaggerate the importance of what one is giving up and to minimize the importance of what one gets in return. Such posturing is part of the game. In most cultures these self-serving negotiating stances are expected, as long as they are kept in decent bounds. [However,] strategic misrepresentation can cause inefficiencies. Consider a distributive bargaining problem in which there is a zone of agreement in actual, but not necessarily in revealed, reservation prices. An inefficiency can arise only if the parties fail to come to an agreement. By bargaining hard the parties may fail to come to an agreement even though any point in the zone of agreement would yield a better outcome for both than the no-agreement state. Still, one cannot conclude from this observation that a negotiator should unilaterally and truthfully reveal his or her reservation price. . . . [N]egotiators [should] act openly and honestly on efficiency concerns; tradeoffs should be disclosed (if the adversary reciprocates), but reservation prices should be kept private. . . . [E]ach negotiator is well advised to behave cooperatively and honestly (for example, by disclosing tradeoffs) in seeking joint gains, but to bargain more toughly when it comes to sharing the jointly created pie.[25]

A Higher Standard

Extreme competitiveness, while a potent tool, can also create ethical conflicts for the negotiator. Consider the following:

> Imagine that you have to choose whether to act nobly or selfishly. If you act nobly you will be helping others at your own expense; if you act selfishly you will be helping yourself at others' expense. Similarly, those others have similar choices. In order to highlight the tension between helping yourself and helping others, let's specify that if all participants act nobly, all do well and the society flourishes; but regardless of how others act, you can always do better for yourself, as measured in tangible rewards (say,

25. Raiffa, *supra* note 5, at 142-144.

53

profits), if you act selfishly — but at the expense of others. Leaving morality aside for the moment, the best tangible reward accrues to you in this asocial game if you act selfishly and all others act nobly. But if all behave that way, all suffer greatly.[26]

Another reason mitigating against dishonesty or like behavior is that it harms the reputation of the negotiator in the long run.

The point to be made here is that negotiators must always be conscious of ethical considerations, must continually look at their behavior in light of such ethics, and must be aware of the well-being of others and of long-term societal interests. If one does so, he might set an example that can positively influence the behavior of others.

Confidentiality

Confidentiality needs to be considered in two different contexts. The first is that whenever a paralegal is present during a negotiation or, while serving as an advocate, negotiates on behalf of a client, the requirement of confidentiality prohibits the paralegal from discussing the client's affairs with others not involved in the negotiation. A paralegal cannot participate in a negotiation session and then go home and tell his spouse or friends about the negotiation. This is a violation of both the attorney's Code of Professional Responsibility and NALA Canon 7.

The second context is litigation. Any negotiations that qualify as settlement discussions cannot be disclosed during trial and are not subject to discovery.

EXERCISES

1. Plan an actual negotiation. Keep a record of all the steps in which you engage during the entire process. Prepare; practice; do the negotiation. Evaluate your performance and evaluate the other party's performance.

2. Observe a legal negotiation, either in person or on videotape, and (1) identify the steps in the process and (2) determine whether or not there were any ethical problems for the negotiators.

---

26. *Id.* at 346.

3. Do an introspective inventory to determine what type of negotiator you are (or do self-analysis in "Negotiator Pro").

4. Recall something you said recently that made another person angry, and reword what you said so that it would be less likely to cause the same response.

5. Talk with a working paralegal or office manager about negotiation and make a list of the professional negotiations he or she describes.

6. Talk with an attorney about negotiation and make a list of the professional negotiations in which the attorney engages.

7. Research rules and statutes in your state regarding the requirement of good faith efforts to settle litigation. Do the same research for case law.

8. Research the issue of confidentiality of settlement negotiations in your jurisdiction.

Negotiation Role Plays

A Family in Crisis (three parties)

Steve and Donna Stone have a daughter who is attending her first year at a public college, located about 150 miles from their home. While tuition is reasonable, the parents, who are separated, are struggling to pay Sara's tuition and room and board. They discover by accident that she is not attending class regularly and is, therefore, doing very poorly in most of her classes. They confront her with this information and a heated conflict ensues, with Sara accusing her parents of violating her privacy and caring more about money than her. The parents, while normally not in agreement these days, join in accusing Sara of wasting their money and her time. After this confrontation, they go their separate ways. The next weekend Sara is due to come home and her parents want to have a further discussion regarding this issue. Sara has generally been able to talk with her parents and wants to continue in college. Therefore, it is in her best interest to talk with her parents and try to explain her situation.

Office Injustices (five parties)

You are part of a paralegal litigation team. There are three attorneys presently working on a substantial civil matter, which is scheduled for arbitration in six months. First on the team is George Hathaway, the lead attorney who will be taking the matter to arbitration. He is considered a good lawyer and a good litigator, but is distant and a workaholic. The second attorney is Susan McDonald, a mature expert in environmental litigation. She is a hard worker, though not as driven as Hathaway. The third member of the litigation team, Rodney Long, is a legal scholar who is a little out of place with the two aggressive litigators. He is respected for his knowledge, but not for his commitment to ADR, which he is constantly urging everyone to consider.

The paralegals on the team are Larry Lomax, Stephanie Strong, Sheila Thompson, and Lorraine Li. Lorraine is the lead paralegal and has been with the firm for many years. She is knowledgeable and hard-working. She sometimes takes abuse from the attorneys and passes it on to the paralegals. She is in charge of work assignments, while also responsible for her own paralegal work. Sheila Thompson appears to be a weak link in the team. She was just hired and is very inexperienced. Her attendance is also a problem and it takes her too long to get the work done. However, the attorneys like her because she is very personable and knows how to stroke their egos. Stephanie has been at the firm for about a year and is a certified paralegal. She is very career-oriented and is a good contributor to the team, but her interpersonal skills are sometimes lacking. Finally, Larry is Mr. Nice Guy. He works hard, but his major asset is his ability to get along with everyone. He is the first African-American in this law firm.

Recently, several issues have arisen to cause dissension on the team: work distribution, overtime, and professional development, i.e., the firm's support of continuing education for the paralegals through payment of tuition, fees for continuing education courses, time off to attend seminars, or professional conferences. Lorraine has responsibility for work distribution, but George Hathaway is the authority on the other matters. Rodney has noticed a morale problem among the paralegals and has suggested a meeting of the team to resolve some of the problems.

The Computer System

The law firm of Long, Tyrol & Kamp is located in the suburbs of Denver, Colorado. They are a relatively young firm that has become well known for their representation of gay activists, fighting for gay employment and health rights. Now others battling discriminatory treatment are beginning to come to them for help and their business is improving.

Jerry Tyne is the paralegal. He has been with the firm almost since its inception and is highly regarded by the three attorneys who make up the firm. He is computer knowledgeable and has been urging the firm to purchase a computer system, which will benefit both the attorneys and him. Pat Long has resisted, probably because she is "computer phobic." However, the other partners and Jerry have finally convinced her. They have assigned Jerry the responsibility of finding the appropriate software and hardware within a given budget. Jerry is thrilled. He puts together an outline of what he believes the firm needs: word processing, electronic mail, docket control, litigation system, deposition reading system, spreadsheet program, communications system, and networking. He contacts a number of firms and gets proposals from each. He has narrowed it down to one company, and is now negotiating price and services.

The company, Compros, will provide five computers, and WordPerfect™ for word processing and electronic mail, a docket control package, a litigation system, a deposition reading system, Lotus™ for spreadsheets, and a communication program to work with the modem. (Jerry would like to see the firm get a subscription to Lexis™ or Westlaw™.) Compros will network the computers to facilitate information sharing.

The Japanese Businessman

The law firm of Carnival, Struts, Styne, and Taylor has begun to expand into the international business arena. Jason Carnival has been serving as an arbitrator in several international business disputes, particularly involving European and Asian transactions. As a result, his reputation in these communities has grown and he recently received an inquiry from a Japanese manufacturing company regarding representation in the United States. After a number of delays and a great deal of "telephone tag," he arranged an appointment with Charles Liu, an attorney from Japan, who represented the company in its country of origin. Mr. Carnival was very excited about the prospect of cultivating this contact with an eye to future legal business.

The appointment was scheduled for last Monday at 10:00 A.M. In anticipation of the meeting, Mr. Carnival spent the week reading whatever he could get his hands on regarding the Japanese business and legal culture. In addition, he spoke to several other attorneys who had experience with Japanese businessmen. He researched the specific company and spent some time on the Internet to further expand his knowledge of the ways in which American and Japanese businessmen and attorneys are similar in their approach to a business meeting and how they differ. Needless to say, he was as prepared as he could be. His paralegal, Joyce Summers, had done some of the research for him and had summarized her findings. She knew how concerned he was that this meeting proceed to establish a long-term arrangement.

The Thursday before the meeting, Mr. Carnival had to fly to Chicago for depositions, which lasted through Friday and Saturday morning. He was scheduled to fly back to Los Angeles on Sunday morning. There was a blizzard in the Midwest on Sunday and no flights were permitted to leave. The airlines were, however, promising that service would be returning to normal at midnight. Therefore, although he was concerned, Mr. Carnival rescheduled his return flight for 1:00 A.M. on Monday.

Meanwhile, back at Carnival, Struts, Styne, and Taylor, the flu was raging through the office personnel. Both his secretary and his paralegal, Ms. Summers, fell ill and were bedridden. By Monday morning there was only a skeleton crew at the law firm. Worse yet, there was a total breakdown of communications; messages left by Mr. Carnival on the receptionist's voice mail, as well as that of his secretary and partners, went unheard. Present in the office at 10:00 A.M. were Joshua Lopez, an associate; Robyn Rosen, Mr. Struts's secretary; Greg Wozniak, a recently hired paralegal; and someone from the word processing department. Ms. Rosen was sitting at the receptionist's desk, frustrated because she was unable to accomplish her own work while answering telephones and dealing with visitors.

When Mr. Liu arrived, Ms. Rosen began a search for Mr. Carnival and finally determined, after about half an hour, that he was still stuck in Chicago. Mr. Liu explained that he was scheduled to fly back to Japan that afternoon and could he at least meet with someone. Ms. Rosen spoke with Mr. Lopez, but he was working on an Order to Show Cause that was scheduled before the judge at 1:00 that afternoon. Lopez apologized, but indicated that it would be impossible to meet with Mr. Liu. Next, Ms. Rosen called Mr. Wozniak to meet with Mr. Liu and they met in his office for about half an hour. After that Mr. Liu left and Mr. Wozniak returned to his work.

On Tuesday morning, when things began to return to normal and Mr. Carnival was able to get a flight home, he called Mr. Wozniak and thanked him for helping out and asked what had been discussed at the meeting. Mr. Wozniak said he had apologized for Mr. Carnival's inadvertent cancellation and that the meeting had been strained, but that Mr. Liu had asked a number of personal questions, followed by some questions about the firm and then left. When Mr. Carnival arrived in the office, he called Mr. Liu in Japan and was told he was not in and would not be available for some time. Mr. Carnival began to get an uneasy feeling, but other work demanded his attention. When he did not receive a return call by Thursday, he called again and was told the same thing. He decided to write to Mr. Liu and also to sit down with Mr. Wozniak, explain some of the things he had learned about the Japanese culture and way of doing business, and find out more specifically what had transpired at the meeting.

Mediation

Introduction

Preparation for Mediation
    Mediator Preparation
    Party Preparation

Methodology
    Community Model
    Business Model
    Single-Text Mediation
    Therapy/Counseling vs. Mediation
    Other Variations

Essential Steps in the Process
    Mediator Introduction
    Party Statements/Factfinding
    Issue Clarification and Option Generation
    Selecting Alternatives/Decisionmaking
    Clarification
    Closing
    Implementation
    Summary

Facilitative Skills
    Communication Skills
    Interpersonal Skills

Neutrality
   What Is It?
   Power Imbalances

Applications
   Community Disputes
   School Mediation
   Criminal Mediation
   Mediation of Civil Matters
   Mediation of Family Matters
   Mediation of Administrative Matters
   Labor Relations
   Construction Mediation
   Environmental Mediation
   Business Mediation
   International Mediation
   Mediation Within Indigenous Communities

Ethics
   Self-Determination
   Impartiality
   Confidentiality
   Conflicts of Interest
   Competence
   Illegal Agreements
   Appropriate Parties and Unrepresented Interests
   Power Imbalances
   Language
   Disclosure of Criminal Activity

Summary

Exercises

Mediation Role Plays
   Neighborhood Dispute
   Women in College
   Corporate Legal Department

Introduction

Mediation is practiced in many forms and in a variety of settings. It is rapidly becoming embedded in our legal system. It is a mode of dispute resolution that introduces a third-party neutral, or a panel of neutrals, to assist the disputing parties in reaching an agreement or settlement.

> The process utilizes a neutral third party . . . to facilitate communication between the disputants, to assist them in defining the issues in dispute, to help them develop options and alternatives, and to reach a consensual resolution that is satisfactory and agreeable to all involved. Mediation as a problem-solving intervention is both goal-directed and issue-oriented. The goals of mediation are the resolution of a dispute and the development of an agreement.[1]

Participation by the disputants in mediation is generally voluntary, although there is sometimes a mandatory orientation meeting to introduce the parties to the process. Occasionally, participation in the entire process is mandated either by contract or by the court. In the latter situation, however, settlement cannot be mandated. The neutral mediator cannot impose a decision on the parties the way an arbitrator or judge does. Rather, the mediator uses a wide range of skills to facilitate communication among the parties looking toward a better understanding of each other's position, a recognition of their own interests, and a resolution of their conflict. "The mediator is a conflict manager and resolution facilitator."[2]

Mediation has been called "facilitated negotiation." It can be a very exciting process for all the parties because it requires disputant participation and an expansion of understanding and communication skills. The parties or disputants are encouraged to be in control of the process, rather than giving up control to a decisionmaker. It is informal and less threatening than a court proceeding and permits the parties to express their feelings, to improve their own communication skills, and to hear the other side of the conflict. This setting, combined with the skills of the mediator and the parties' desire to end the conflict, helps to bring the disputants into an agreement that resolves their conflict. It is not surprising, therefore, that studies indicate that a mediated agreement is more likely to be complied with than one imposed by a judge or arbitrator.

1. Samuel G. Forlenza, Mediation and Psychotherapy: Parallel Processes, *in* Community Mediation: A Handbook for Practitioners and Researchers 228 (Karen Duffy et al. eds., 1991) (citations omitted).
2. *Id.* at 230.

For mediation to be successful, disputants sometimes have to alter their perspective. In the United States, we are a very competitive people and place a high premium on "winning." In approaching mediation, "[t]he important consideration is not who is 'right' and therefore 'wins' but rather what is the solution that meets the needs of the problem and with which the disputants can live."[3]

In a mediation, the parties, and sometimes their representatives, meet with the mediator(s) to discuss the dispute. Each participant has an opportunity to "tell his side of the story." The parties are told to be respectful, to not interrupt each other, and to not engage in other openly hostile behavior, such as name-calling. If the mediator thinks it appropriate, she can meet with each party individually (caucus) to examine his interests and positions and to better understand his side of the conflict. Disputants, too, sometimes find it easier to speak privately to a neutral and are willing to let the neutral speak on their behalf to the other parties in order to communicate their desires. No information obtained in the caucus, however, can be communicated to the other party without permission of the individual with whom she caucused.

Through this process of direct and indirect communication, the parties come to a better understanding of their own needs, the other parties' needs, and the value of creating their own solution. This ultimately brings them closer to a solution.

Preparation for Mediation

Mediator Preparation

There are many instances where the mediator has no knowledge of the facts or circumstances of the conflict prior to meeting with the parties. In those situations, the mediator is obviously unable to do any factual preparation. However, a good mediator will at least prepare and practice an introduction/opening statement and provide a comfortable, nonthreatening environment for the mediation.

In business mediation, particularly through the American Arbitration Association, the parties can submit a Statement of Claim or a Notice of Intent to Mediate and an Answer; these are informal equivalents

3. Andrea Nager Chasen, Defining Mediation and Its Use for Paralegals, 9. J. Paralegal Edu. & Prac. 64 (1993).

of pleadings. The mediator will read all such material submitted by the parties prior to the first meeting.

In some mediation practices, the parties have met extensively with someone from the mediation center as part of the intake process prior to formal mediation. This can result in the mediator commencing the mediation session with a greater knowledge of the dispute. Whatever degree of information the mediator has available to him, he should familiarize himself with it prior to the mediation session.

It should be noted, however, that there is a difference of opinion in the field as to whether the mediator should be familiar with the facts and positions of the parties prior to mediation. Some believe that when the mediator possesses such information, she can expedite the mediation and minimize the partie's, getting entrenched when stating their positions. Others believe that the mediator should go into the mediation with a clean slate and without any preconceived ideas based on submissions by the parties. Further, these theorists argue that when parties prepare pre-mediation filings, they become committed to particular positions and are less amenable to looking at interests underlying those positions and thereby working toward resolution.

Party Preparation

The parties prepare for a mediation in the same way they prepare for a negotiation. (See Chapter 3, at pages 39-40.) They critically analyze and evaluate their own issues, as well as obtain all possible information about other disputants' issues. They consider their best alternative to a negotiated agreement (BATNA).[4] They determine their optimum and least desirable, but acceptable, result. In so doing, they produce a range in which settlement is acceptable to them. While role-playing is not as easy in preparing for mediation as it is in negotiation preparation, it can still be beneficial. At a minimum, the parties can prepare their own written positions, so that when they have the opportunity to speak at the mediation, they can be clear and precise and not omit any important issues. Such a written preparation can also aid in overcoming nervousness at the mediation.

---

4. See Roger Fisher et al., Getting to Yes 99, 100 (2d ed. 1991). See also chapter 3, at page 40.

Methodology

The role of the mediator is the major differentiating factor in the following mediation models.

> There is a continuum of roles, from weak to strong, that a mediator can play. On the weak side, the mediator may be just a convener of meetings or a nonsubstantive, neutral discussion leader; he or she might simply maintain rules of civilized debate or occasionally give a reticent speaker a chance to interject some comments.[5]

On the stronger side of the continuum, mediators are more participatory and suggest solutions and urge agreement.

Community Model

In the community model, the mediator is a facilitator and does very little to suggest resolutions to the parties. He encourages brainstorming, reality testing, and increased communication among the parties to bring them to their own settlement. The benefit of this model is that it permits the exploration and expression of emotions and the parties are better able to develop their own solution. This process, however, can be time-consuming and thus may be inappropriate in a setting where time constraints are an issue.

Proponents of this model strongly favor the nondirective mediator role as providing the better chance at reaching a lasting resolution of the dispute. "Although research on mediation styles is in its infancy, there is some evidence that the more active or controlling mediators achieve higher rates of settlement, but that these agreements are more likely to collapse over time."[6]

Business Model

Another type of mediation, more likely to be used in settling business or commercial disputes, is one in which the mediator is a more active participant in both suggesting resolutions and urging acceptance of

5. Howard Raiffa, The Art & Science of Negotiation 218 (1982).
6. Linda R. Singer, Settling Disputes: Conflict Resolution in Business, Families, and The Legal System 40 (2d ed. 1994).

resolutions. Here, the mediator's knowledge of the subject matter of the dispute is often valuable. Consider a dispute over construction issues, for example, where the disputants are both business people and want a neutral who will be informed, be able to understand their conflict, and actively assist them in their discussions, debates, and, ultimately, their creation of an agreement. "The more complex and controversial the issue, the more likely it is that the mediators will become actively involved."[7]

When attorneys or the court system are involved in a mediation process, this more active mediation technique is likely to be used. Rather than looking at underlying issues, the court system is more concerned with the dispute at hand and its settlement.

Single-Text Mediation

Utilizing a single text (see Chapter 3, at page 38) is a mediation method that focuses on one proffered resolution, which the parties modify until they are satisfied. In this way, the parties are led to concentrate on the vehicle for solution, not their individual differences. This approach is particularly useful in mediation because "[t]he mediator . . . prepare[s] a single negotiating text and then successively modifies it after the disputants have criticized it separately and collectively. . . ."[8]

Therapy/Counseling vs. Mediation

Traditionally, a distinction is made between mediation and psychotherapy or counseling. Certainly they do share some common attributes, and there is a place for certain therapeutic techniques in the mediation process. However, dispute resolution professionals stress that therapy and mediation are different processes and should not be confused. "The role of counselors often is to facilitate ongoing and in-depth exploration of personal issues, with the goal of dealing with problems rooted in the past. For a mediation to occur, there must be a discrete dispute."[9]

7. *Id.* at 149.
8. Raiffa, *supra* note 5, at 220.
9. Selma Myers & Barbara Filner, Mediation Across Cultures — A Handbook About Conflict and Culture 20 (1993) (citations omitted).

The dispute resolution process does not dwell on the history of the conflict, but rather looks to see what may be done in the present to change future events. Mediation is concerned with the past to the extent that such a focus may aid the parties to develop a workable solution. Feelings are controlled and directed in mediation. The criterion is the furthering of the dispute resolution. If the expression of emotions can be channeled to facilitate this process, such expression is then considered useful and productive. Effective mediation views ventilation to have a significant but more limited role. In contrast to psychotherapy, conflict management does not and cannot permit this free and unrestricted exploration. Although feelings cannot be ignored, their containment and redirection seem to be most useful in promoting agreement, which of course is the goal of mediation.[10]

Other Variations

Practitioners will discover that there are many variations on these models, as well as other mediation or conflict resolution paradigms.[11] Co-mediation, for example, utilizes two or more mediators as neutrals. This can affect the way disputants align themselves, but it also provides the opportunity to ensure greater diversity as to race, gender, and profession (attorney and therapist) in the co-mediator role.

A mediator needs to be sensitive to the needs of the parties and the organizational structure in which she works to determine which mediation model is best suited for each case. Some parties will be unable to function within the framework of the existing model of mediation; therefore, mediation will fail if the mediator is insensitive to this issue or unable to fashion a more acceptable model. Some sponsoring organizations will permit flexibility and others will not.

It should be noted here that one of the goals of the mediation process is an agreement between the parties. Obviously, this is not always attained, although a significant number of mediated cases do result in settlement. Even among those that do not settle, however, the parties generally walk away with an appreciation of the mediation process and a better understanding of their conflict.[12]

---

10. Forlenza, *supra* note 1, at 231-232.

11. For example, some mediators participate in a form of advocacy mediation where they "represent" or advocate for one of the parties. Most scholars, however, would reject such a model because it jeopardizes the neutrality of the mediator.

12. See Craig McEwen and Richard J. Maiman, Small Claims Mediation in Maine: An Empirical Assessment, *in* Stephen B. Goldberg et al., Dispute Resolution: Negotiation, Mediation, and Other Processes 148-155 (1992).

Essential Steps in the Process

One must first understand that mediation, like negotiation, can involve a single issue or multiple issues, two parties or multiple parties. The process can be completed in as little as half an hour, or it can extend over a year or more, with periodic lengthy meetings. The subject matter can be a neighborhood dispute over a barking dog, or it can comprise a large environmental dispute with the logging industry, the environmentalists, and the community each having a different vested interest in the resolution. Mediation can be mandated by a contract between the parties, be required as a precondition for litigation, or be voluntarily agreed upon by the parties. Mediation services are provided by individuals in private mediation practice, through dispute resolution organizations, such as Endispute and the American Arbitration Association, through community or school organizations, or under the auspices of the courts. Mediators include attorneys, mental health professionals, individuals with specific subject matter expertise, and laypeople. Paralegals will find opportunities to mediate in community justice centers, some municipal courts, the Better Business Bureau, or within a private mediation practice.

Where to locate the beginning of the mediation process is not so easy. In some settings, the first step of initial intake is when information is gathered and filed for the mediator's benefit. The parties may then receive an introductory description of the process. In other situations, intake is the filing of a complaint and answer. In still others, intake is the filing of a request for mediation. However, regardless of these variations as to the initial intake, the mediator is usually not involved in this opening step and we will therefore commence our analysis of the process with the mediator's opening statement.

Mediator Introduction

In an introductory session or orientation, the mediator reviews the process and the rules to the parties. The mediator explains her role, the fact that she does not make any binding determination, and that any resolution reached will be the decision of the parties. She describes confidentiality and its impact on the process and explains that she may want to caucus, or meet privately, with each party during the mediation. A new mediator may want to keep a checklist of what should be included in the mediator's introduction. (See the checklist at page 73.)

69

The mediator answers any questions the parties may have and attempts to make them feel comfortable. She will ask the parties to agree to certain behavioral constraints, such as not interrupting each other, not calling each other names, being respectful of each other and the mediator, no smoking, etc. When the orientation is completed, the mediator should confirm the parties' understanding. Sometimes the parties are asked to sign a contract agreeing to the rules and committing to the process. (See appendix E.)

Party Statements/Factfinding

The mediation then proceeds to fact gathering. Usually the party that brought the conflict to the mediation is asked to "tell his story" first, with the other individual responding when the "complainant" is finished. This order is not mandatory, however, and the mediator can ask either party to start. In a multi-party mediation, each party should have the opportunity to present his issues. If multiple issues are disputed, the mediator and the parties may work out an agenda prioritizing the issues. If the parties are able to communicate in each other's presence, then open discussions can begin regarding the issues.

Issue Clarification and Option Generation

The process of factfinding will generally carry over into this next segment of the mediation, just as issue clarification usually begins when the party statements are given. However, in this third phase of mediation, the parties are guided beyond what has happened in the past and are encouraged to look to the future and at what they want to have happen or not happen. To do so, the mediator keeps the parties focused on the issues in dispute and how to resolve them, not on the prior injustices that brought them to mediation in the first place.

The mediator helps the parties express themselves if necessary. This can be done by repeating what each party says in a nonjudgmental fashion or assisting each in caucus to verbalize her interests. When it appears that an impasse has been reached, the mediator keeps the process going by moving on to another issue, breaking the tension by calling a break or telling a joke, or facilitating more creative problem solving.

It is the function of the mediator to create an environment where the parties volunteer their own suggestions for solutions. This may require the mediator initially to request such suggestions for resolution from the parties and to affirmatively explore any suggestions that are made. In a particularly uninhibited environment, the parties are encouraged to brainstorm, which permits individuals to offer any ideas they may have regarding solutions without fear as to how those ideas would be judged. This encourages the free flow of ideas and opens up the opportunity for creative thinking. Ultimately, the parties are encouraged by the mediator to seek joint gains.

Selecting Alternatives/Decisionmaking

In this step of the process, the mediator does reality testing with all parties and explores nonagreement options. Reality testing directs the parties to look critically at their own positions and decide whether they are being practical in their demands. This is accomplished by the mediator's asking each party questions about the merits of their position. Exploring nonagreement options and determining a party's BATNA (see page 40) are part of reality testing. The parties must determine, as best they are able, what will happen if they do not reach an agreement. Will there be litigation? What will litigation cost — economically, emotionally, and in lost time? What is the risk factor, i.e., is a judge likely to decide in their favor? If the judge does decide in their favor, will they be able to collect the judgment amount? Is there an ongoing relationship with the other party that will be destroyed in litigation?

These techniques can be used either in a joint meeting with all parties present or in caucus. The mediator's skill is in encouraging the parties themselves to explore alternative settlement options, which provides them the opportunity to choose one that can best meet the needs of all parties. Through this process, the parties can reach a tentative agreement.

Clarification

Once the facts are gathered, options generated, and the best alternative selected, the mediator must pause and make sure that the parties understand all the terms of the tentative agreement. Beginning mediators are fearful of this step because it may give the disputants an opportunity to rehash their conflict. However, it is essential that all parties understand and agree to the terms of the resolution. Some mediators ask the parties to state in their own words the terms of the agreement so that the mediator can make it part of the written mediation agreement.

Closing

In the closing, the agreement between the parties is confirmed and sometimes committed to writing. Most solutions should be written and signed by the parties, although in some situations they may first want to consult others before signing a formal agreement. The basics of the agreement should be recorded in some manner, however, to ensure that all parties agree to and understand it. In a court program, the parties will sometimes appear before a judge to finalize their agreement in the form of a judgment or court order. In divorce mediation, the parties' agreement becomes the basis for a separation agreement. A word of caution here: Some states prohibit the mediator from drafting an agreement in a divorce mediation. Therefore, one must be aware of the regulations and ethical constraints in various jurisdictions.

Some authorities emphasize the value of emotional closure as well, which can be some sort of ceremonial gesture such as a handshake or sharing a cup of coffee. What is deemed appropriate will depend on the nature of the conflict and its setting.

Implementation

If the conflict is a public one, the agreement may need public acceptance. Part of the closing may therefore include the development of a plan for public presentation, acceptance, implementation, and monitoring of the agreement. The mediator can also serve the function of publicly articulating the rationale for the agreement. Other agreements may require the mediators to oversee the implementation phase. Regardless of whether the mediator is involved, the manner in which the agreement will be carried out must be clearly stated and understood, with as much detail as possible or necessary. It may require that the parties meet again with the mediator for future communication.[13]

Summary of Essential Steps for Mediators

The following checklist can be a useful guide.

---

13. For other approaches to the steps of mediation, see Kimberlee K. Kovach, Mediation, Principles, and Practice 26 (1994).

Mediator Introduction

1. Introduce self and qualifications.
2. Explain neutrality.
3. Explain the mediation process, including the caucus.
4. Explain the ground rules, i.e., no interrupting, name-calling, etc.
5. Set the tone and tenor and build trust with parties.
6. Explain role as mediator, i.e., not a decisionmaker.
7. Explain the benefits of mediation and show enthusiasm for process.
8. Seek commitment from disputants to mediate in good faith.
9. Thoroughly explain the concept and applicability of confidentiality (and its exceptions, if any).
10. Ask the disputants if they have any questions.
11. Identify any potential conflicts of interest.
12. Reinforce parties' participation or attendance.
13. Explain who goes first and why.
14. Go over "housekeeping" details.
15. Determine whether there are representatives and establish the degree of their participation.
16. Explain possible need for taking notes.

Party Statements/Factfinding

1. Identify order of speaking.
2. Demonstrate or model good listening skills.
3. Make sure only one person speaks at a time.
4. Make sure parties have relatively equal time to speak.
5. Reword judgmental language used by parties.
6. Assess suitability for mediation.
7. Help parties prioritize issues if appropriate.

Issue Clarification and Option Generation

1. Ask the parties what each is seeking from the mediation.
2. Reinforce points of agreement and determine points of disagreement.
3. Analyze problem in order to ask effective questions.
4. Engage in reality testing at the appropriate time.

5. Ask effective questions intended to obtain necessary information.
6. Focus parties on issues and away from positions.
7. Use the caucus effectively.
8. Ask the parties to put themselves in the other's shoes.
9. Encourage creative problem solving.
10. Clarify or summarize solutions as they are presented.

Selecting Alternatives/Decisionmaking

1. Suggest use of objective criteria.
2. Stress shared interests.
3. Discuss BATNA (not necessary to use words, but use concept).
4. Do reality testing if appropriate.
5. Encourage principled negotiation.
6. Encourage parties to make suggestions for resolution.
7. Avoid exerting inappropriate pressure to resolve dispute.
8. Avoid giving professional (legal) advice.

Clarification

1. Clarify agreement.
2. Affirm that it is the parties' agreement.
3. Confirm that the parties thoroughly understand all elements of the agreement.

Closing

1. Write agreement (if appropriate).
2. Have parties sign agreement.
3. Refer parties to counsel (if appropriate).
4. Leave door open for future conflict resolution.
5. Close mediation session comfortably.

Generally

1. Demonstrate knowledge of process.
2. Act interested.
3. Appear to be in control of the process.

4. Encourage appropriate direct communication between the parties.
5. Use neutral language.
6. Demonstrate calming skills when necessary.
7. Demonstrate patience.
8. Keep parties future-oriented.
9. Permit appropriate venting.
10. Demonstrate sensitivity to which issues need resolution and which do not.

Facilitative Skills

Communication Skills

Well-developed communication skills are essential in negotiation and mediation. Foremost among them is the ability to communicate in a nonjudgmental fashion in order to maintain the appearance of neutrality. This is often difficult for those with legal training, as the tendency is to look at conflicts from a right/wrong, win/lose perspective. At a minimum, lawyers and paralegals tend to view disputes from the perspective of asking who is "liable" or who is most likely to be successful in court. As mediators, they must keep in mind that they are facilitators, not decisionmakers or advocates. Nonjudgmental communication requires the use of neutral language,[14] as well as neutral nonverbal communication. Unless consciously used as a device to help bring the parties to agreement, the mediator should avoid all facial expressions and body movements that convey surprise, shock, dismay, disbelief, and similar emotion.

The second most important communication skill is the ability to concentrate and listen attentively to each party. This has a number of beneficial consequences. First, each party to a dispute wants someone to listen to them and hear their side of the story. A mediator should look at each individual as she is speaking, listen to what she is saying, and acknowledge what she has said. Such active listening creates a positive environment and makes the party feel affirmed. Second, if the mediator listens carefully, he may pick up a clue as to how the conflict can be settled. The parties know the dispute better than the mediator and probably have thought about how it could be resolved. Listen for the parties' solutions. Third, the mediator serves as a model for an active listener. By

14. See chapter 3, at page 46.

demonstrating active listening, the mediator serves as a role model and contributes to each party hearing and understanding the position of the other.[15]

Finally, the mediator must be able to reword what a party has said in a nonjudgmental, nonthreatening fashion. This skill allows the mediator to confirm that she understood what the party said; and by repeating it, she is making sure that the other party understands it too. Because the mediator repeats the party's statement in a nonjudgmental manner, she can take the "sting" out of it. This tactic is not required with every communication; however, when the parties are not understanding each other, it is a powerful tool.

Interpersonal Skills

To aid the parties in reaching an agreement, the mediator leads the parties beyond their stated positions and inquires as to their underlying interests and encourages them to recognize those interests and to verbalize them. The mediator assists the parties in thinking creatively about solutions to their conflict. The mediator may question the parties' positions, inquire about the costs of litigation, and recommend the benefits of mediation and the settlement process. Finally, the mediator gives the parties face-saving methods to enable them to move off of their positions, without losing face in front of the other party.

If the parties are locked in a stalemate, the mediator can help move them to another issue. If the parties keep arguing about past injustices, the mediator can help them focus on the future and the possible solution. If the mediation does not produce an agreement, he can leave the door open for future discussions. Finally, the mediator can assist the parties in drafting the agreement that they reach.

A final note on style. The mediator has his or her own well-developed personality. It is not suggested that the mediator change his or her personal style. Rather, the mediator should be aware of how that style affects other people and should be flexible enough to modify it if a situation requires. For example, some mediators have very affable and outgoing personalities and will maintain a very positive, relaxed mediation environment. Others are more quiet, restrained, and observant; they tend to create a more professional atmosphere. If the more outgoing mediator is dealing with two very restrained parties, they may find her approach too intrusive. She needs to be aware of this, be flexible, and try to maintain an atmosphere that is comfortable for the parties involved.

15. For specific techniques, see chapter 3 at pages 46-47.

On the other hand, a more restrained mediator may seem cold and uninterested to a party who is very outgoing, and she likewise must be aware of this and be willing to modify her approach to create greater comfort for the disputants.

Neutrality

What Is It?

Neutrality in mediation is the ability to moderate between individuals in conflict without demonstrating bias in favor of or against any disputant or their interests. While no one can be completely neutral, it is extremely important to remain as neutral as possible when serving as a mediator. It is not the mediator's position to judge the case, the parties, or their actions, except as to behavior that negatively affects the mediation process. It is the parties' dispute and they will create their own solution, with the mediator's assistance and guidance.

The mediator may find that he dislikes one or both of the parties. It is essential, however, that his demeanor and language remain nonjudgmental. If the mediator finds it impossible to remain neutral and the parties or their conflict engenders very strong feelings or reactions in the mediator, it is best to withdraw as the mediator. To do otherwise would be a disservice to the process and the disputants.

To remain neutral requires constant vigilance on the part of the mediator. "Value systems are filled to overflowing with prejudices, opinions, and pre-conceived ideas. Constant vigilance is required so as to not manipulate disputants to a settlement according to what mediators think it should be."[16]

As indicated in the section on communication skills (page 75), retaining the appearance of neutrality through nonjudgmental communication, both verbal and nonverbal, is vital.

Power Imbalances

A secondary issue in neutrality is dealing effectively with power imbalances between the disputants. It may appear to the mediator that

16. Charles A. Kerr, In Mediation What Am I?, The Alternative Dispute Resolution Center of Snohomish and Island Counties, Everett, Washington (Spring 1993).

there is a serious power difference between the parties. The first step is to determine whether that is the mediator's perception or whether there is in fact a serious power imbalance between the parties. The meek, quiet person is not always weak. Nor is the loud boisterous person always strong. The second step is to determine whether the power imbalance will adversely affect the mediation.

Some writers in this area believe that a mediator should not attempt to balance the distribution of power between parties because that would influence his neutrality or appearance of neutrality. Others say, however, that some power imbalances can be dealt with by having the parties consult counsel or other support, or by deeply questioning the "weaker" person to encourage them to play a stronger role. The latter is usually done in caucus.

Any attempt by the mediator to balance the power between parties must proceed with care, particularly in interpersonal disputes where the parties' relationship will continue after the mediation. This relationship existed prior to the mediator's intervention and will continue afterwards, without the intervention of the mediator. A mediator should be mindful of this.

Applications

Mediation is not the magic solution for all conflicts. While some proponents believe mediation should be utilized for all cases, most agree that mediation is effective when at least one of the following criteria is present: where there is an ongoing relationship, business or personal, between the parties; where more than just the disputants need to participate, i.e., children, teachers, etc.; where flexibility in process and/or agreement is needed; where privacy is important; or where the disputants do not wish to set precedents. Situations in which mediation is less likely to be successful are where there are clashing values or principles; where a party wants to be vindicated; where there is a history of violence between the parties; or where a party is abusing drugs or alcohol. These sets of criteria describe conflicts that are at opposite ends of the spectrum, and there are many disputes that fall in between and would be amenable to mediation.

As indicated in the beginning of this chapter, mediation has been used to resolve a broad range of disputes. They could be categorized in a number of ways, but here they are arranged by the subject matter of the dispute. Some of these categories necessarily overlap.

Community Disputes

Disputes at the local level can involve seemingly minor issues between community members, such as an individual playing her radio loudly or not controlling the behavior of her children. However, built-up frustration sometimes exaggerates such disputes and results in violence if the problem is not addressed. These are the types of conflicts that find their way into municipal or small claims court or community justice centers. Today many courts are introducing mediation as an alternative to dispute resolution to settle such community disputes.

Sometimes, however, neighborhood disputes are not even the type of problem that can be handled by a court. "Realistically, a large portion of the conflicts brought to dispute centers never would have appeared in court. Either prosecutors would not have bothered to bring charges in many of the less serious cases between family members or neighbors, or there would have been no effective judicial remedy."[17] Across the nation, Community Mediation Centers have sprung up over the last 15 years to handle such disputes.[18] Mediators in community centers and at the lower court levels are frequently volunteer laypeople.

The mediation of a layperson may not be enough when community groups are in deep conflict, such as when the police department and the residents of a particular neighborhood dispute allegations of unwarranted police force. In those cases, an outside professional mediator frequently is brought in to lessen tensions, explore the problems and their sources, and develop a long-term plan to resolve those problems.

School Mediation

Teaching children and young people to mediate their conflicts is a rapidly growing area of education. The Conflict Resolution Education Network at NIDR[19] is an organization that actively supports integrating mediation into the school systems, from elementary school through college. School mediation involves training students to serve as peer mediators when a conflict arises between other students. Such school mediation programs have proven successful in helping students to develop new skills and "to reduce school violence, to provide an alterna-

---

17. Singer, *supra* note 6, at 117.
18. *Id.* at 111.
19. More information about Conflict Resolution Education Network is available by writing 1726 M Street, NW Suite 500, Washington, DC 20036-4502.

tive to suspension, and, perhaps most importantly, to help students learn ways of responding to conflict other than by fighting or dropping out."[20]

Some teacher education programs now train teachers in mediation techniques so that they can pass these skills on to their students.[21]

The establishment of school conflict resolution programs and peer mediation programs at the elementary and secondary levels is a fast-growing phenomenon. Paralegals trained in mediation and conflict resolution can be very helpful in working with their local school district to implement such programs.

Criminal Mediation

Although not as popular as community mediation, criminal mediation can take a number of forms, including victim offender confrontations and mediation of domestic violence.[22]

In still another adaptation of community mediation by the courts, convicted juvenile delinquents in a number of states and adults convicted of crimes in Oklahoma are participating in mediation with their victims to work out mutually acceptable sentences to be recommended jointly to the judge. In most of these programs both the defendant and the victim, who may be a representative of a store or other business, must volunteer for mediation. Mediators are community volunteers or, occasionally, probation or parole officers.

Agreements generally include some sort of restitution to the victim, in the form of money or services, or service to the community instead of or in addition to imprisonment. Offenses for which sentences have been mediated range from burglary and drunk driving to armed assault and manslaughter. Both victims and offenders report satisfaction with the process, with victims saying they appreciated the opportunity to describe directly to the offender how the crime changed their lives and to suggest their own remedies.[23]

Mediation of Civil Matters

Within the court system, mediation of civil law suits covers a broad range of topics at both the state and federal levels. The federal courts

---

20. Singer, *supra* note 6, at 155.

21. Such a program exists at Columbia Teachers College, New York City.

22. Many women's rights activists are strongly opposed to mediation of domestic violence.

23. Singer, *supra* note 6, at 128.

have encouraged mediation through court rules. A recent article in *Dispute Resolution Journal* indicated that "[a]t least 46 states and some 1,200 courts now have some form of official ADR program in place."[24]

In some jurisdictions, mediation is being used for cases that are on appeal, so mediation need not be limited to the trial level.

Mediation of Family Matters

Although domestic issues generally are covered under civil law, family mediation is an area requiring separate treatment. Divorce mediation is done by private mediators as well as through the court system. Both attorneys and mental health professionals serve in this area to develop a settlement agreement that can be incorporated into a judgment of divorce. Many court systems also mandate mediation of at least a portion of a divorce matter, such as child custody and visitation. Mediation of postjudgment disputes is particularly important.

Intra-family disputes are mediated as well, generally through the local community centers. "Conflict within families, whether they occur between parents and teens over adjusting to clashing lifestyles, between adult siblings over caring for elderly parents, or between separating spouses over children or property, spotlight most vividly the advantages and occasional pitfall of negotiated or mediated settlements."[25] Other examples of potential family-oriented conflict include will contests, disagreement over jointly owned property, and the breaking up of a family business. It is clear that such conflicts can be heavily laden with emotional as well as legal issues. And because there is often an ongoing relationship to be considered, mediation would appear to be the most appropriate process for seeking a mutually arrived at settlement.

Mediation of Administrative Matters

Administrative matters are those that come before administrative agencies and administrative courts, both state and federal. Mediation is a part of this process as well. The Americans with Disabilities Act and Equal Employment Opportunity Act are two examples of legislation that provide for mediation.

---

24. Dick S. Gale, ADR at the Crossroads, 49 Disp. Resol. J. (March 1994).
25. Singer, *supra* note 6, at 31.

Similarly,

[p]arents and school administrators are using mediation to deal with disagreements over educating handicapped children. . . . The purpose: to
avoid costly, time-consuming, and emotionally draining administrative
hearings that are permitted annually under the Education for All Handicapped Children Act. . . . Although no form of dispute settlement other
than court or formal administrative hearings is mentioned in the statute, a
growing number of states are devoting significant resources to mediating
disputes over special education.[26]

Labor Relations

Many people think that arbitration is the preferred method of conflict resolution in labor disputes. But the area of labor relations is changing, and the old ways of resolving disputes is giving way to mediation.
Because of its flexibility and maintenance of relationships between the
disputing parties, mediation is an area growing in recognition. Labor relations provides an ADR arena that involves many nonlawyers as neutrals
who have specialty training in labor issues.

Construction Mediation

Construction is another field previously dominated by arbitration.
However, as more contracts contain mediation clauses and more participants convey their satisfaction with nonadjudicative processes, construction mediation will continue to grow. As in labor, the neutral is most
likely a specialist in the construction field rather than an attorney. This
industry is also utilizing a modified version of mediation called "partnering," in which the two parties collaborate to resolve the problems
they have in common. (See "Building Success for the 21st Century: A
Guide to Partnering in the Construction Industry." American Arbitration Association (1996).

Environmental Mediation

This highly public area of conflict has found mediation particularly
appropriate. Large environmental disputes are frequently multi-partied,
multi-issued, and lengthy. One of the goals is to give as many interested
constituents as possible the opportunity to participate in the process and

26. Singer, *supra* note 6, at 157.

the development of a resolution. Such a resolution may be one that the court would have difficulty creating and enforcing. The mediator may be a nonlawyer, but she is frequently someone with specialized expertise in environmental issues.

Business Mediation

"A 1985 guide for business executives with legal disputes termed mediation the 'sleeping giant' of business dispute resolution, potentially the most powerful means of bringing the parties to terms."[27] It has been stated, however, that the best time to mediate business disputes is in the early stages of the conflict, "before disagreements have escalated, before disputants have incurred the costs of preparing a case for trial, perhaps even before they have hired lawyers."[28]

The types of issues that result in conflict in the business setting include conflicts within partnerships, complaints by minority shareholders of closely held corporations, takeovers of smaller business by large corporate acquirers, policy conflicts, and personnel conflicts. Again, mediation is particularly appropriate because it affords privacy, flexibility, and cost containment. Moreover, and perhaps most importantly, it permits the business relationship to continue.

International Mediation

Historians and political scientists can describe numerous settlements of international disputes, both public and private, aided by mediation. Among the issues dealt with by international mediation are border disputes, trade considerations, and long-standing international conflicts. One of the most prominent international mediations was the Camp David meetings and resultant accord.[29] Diplomats and other governmental officials are trained in dispute resolution techniques, and former President Jimmy Carter has established a Center that focuses on international conflict resolution.

Mediation Within Indigenous Communities

Scholarly research on native communities both in North America as well as on the African Continent reveals a long history of forms of me-

27. Singer, *supra* note 6, at 70 (citation omitted).
28. *Id.* at 75.
29. Raiffa, *supra* note 5, at 205-217.

diation. Many indigenous communities have internal justice systems similar to mediation and, as a result, find it the most acceptable aspect of the American justice system.[30]

Ethics

The American Bar Association (ABA) has enacted standards to govern lawyers serving as family mediators, and several other organizations of neutrals have developed their own standards. The Standards of Conduct for Mediators in Appendix A (page 155) were developed by the ABA, the American Arbitration Association (AAA), and the Society for Professionals in Dispute Resolution (SPIDR). They stress the need for self-determination of the parties, impartiality of the neutral, maintaining confidentiality, avoiding conflicts of interest, and providing competent mediators.

Self-Determination

The parties must be able to participate fully in the process and reach a voluntary, uncoerced agreement. In mandatory mediation, which is a prerequisite to proceeding with a court action, generally the mandate applies to an orientation session explaining the process but does not require participation in the process.

Impartiality

The mediator must remain impartial, evenhanded, and avoid even the appearance of partiality toward either of the parties. Such impartiality requires avoiding mediator prejudice based on race, color, creed, national origin, age, sex, and sexual orientation.[31]

Confidentiality

The parties should discuss their expectations of confidentiality and establish what level of confidentiality they wish maintained. Absent an

---

30. Robert D. Garrett, Mediation in Native America, 49 Disp. Resol. J. 38 (March 1994).

31. Standards of Conduct for Mediators §II (see Appendix A at page 155).

agreement to the contrary, or a legal exception, most people assume that everything stated during a mediation should remain confidential and not available to the public. In addition, the parties need to be informed regarding the function and confidentiality of the caucus (private sessions). Anything that is said in a caucus cannot be revealed to other parties without the consent of the party with whom the mediator caucuses.

Confidentiality restrictions apply to the parties and the mediator.

> Courts faced with the issue generally have concluded that mediators need not testify. They have based their reasoning either on the long tradition (often incorporated into court rules) providing confidentiality for settlement offers or on the threatened danger to neutrality if the mediator should be forced to testify for one of the parties.[32]

In a case questioning whether communications were privileged, *Garstang v. Cat Tech,* 46 Cal. Rptr. 2d 84 (1995), the California Court of Appeals determined that communications made to an ombudsperson in a mediation session were protected by qualified privilege pursuant to the California constitutional right to privacy. Therefore, such statements were not subject to discovery in subsequent litigation. "Private institutions have a qualified privilege not to disclose communications made before an ombudsman in an attempt to mediate an employee dispute."[33] The court rejected the contention that the communications were privileged because they occurred during a mediation, but rather based the privilege on a right to privacy weighed against compelling public need for discovery. This should give comfort to ombudsmen, if not to mediators.

Conflicts of Interests

A mediator is required to disclose to the parties any actual or potential conflicts of interest that she may have with the parties. If the parties wish to continue with that mediator after being so informed, the mediation can proceed, unless the nature of the conflict of interest itself casts serious doubt on the integrity of the process. For example, even though a mediator may know one of the parties professionally, the mediation may still proceed if the parties do not object. If, however, the mediation is between a physician and a dissatisfied patient over possible malpractice and the mediator had previously been a patient of the physician, that relationship creates too strong an impression of possible bias. A mediator should also avoid any subsequent relationship with a party.

32. Singer, *supra* note 6, at 175 (*citing* NLRB v. Macaluso, 618 F.2d 51 (9th Cir. 1980)).
33. 46 Cal. Rptr. 2d at 89.

A mediator must be sensitive to the fact that her employing agency wants to demonstrate high settlement statistics to justify the continued use of mediation. Further, the mediator's own drive to succeed may pressure her to settle as many cases as possible. However, the mediator must take care that these types of conflicts of interest do not interfere with her professionalism and commitment to the parties' self-determination.

Competence

The degree and formality of training for mediators and supervision of the mediation process are not settled issues. Education and experience, both in the dispute resolution process and sometimes in the subject matter of the dispute, are very important and must be considered in the selection of a mediator. Unfortunately, the public is not well informed regarding mediator qualifications and may not be in a position to make an informed choice.

The parties' informed choice of a mediator and their satisfaction with the mediator's qualifications is part of the goal of self-determination in alternative dispute resolution. In court-administered or court-referred programs, the court regulates the training and educational requirements of the mediator. Unless there is state licensing, however, anyone can offer to mediate a conflict privately outside of the court system. It is therefore incumbent upon the mediator to truthfully inform the public as to her qualifications and to refuse to participate in any mediation for which she believes herself to be unprepared or unqualified to mediate.

Another concern is the ongoing supervision and continuing education of mediators. Mediation is a private process, observed only by the neutral and the parties. Since the parties are generally unsophisticated regarding the process, they may be unable to judge the quality of the intervening neutral. Mediators should participate in periodic continuing education and supervised mediation. This will help the mediator overcome the sense of isolation that she experiences and cause her to refine her skills, avoid bad habits, and learn new areas or techniques. If paralegals and lawyers are encouraged, and sometimes required, to participate in continuing education, mediators should be as well.

Illegal Agreements

What does a mediator do when he realizes that the parties have reached a solution that is either illegal or against public policy? Examples of an illegal agreement would be divorcing parties' agreeing to call alimony child support for tax benefits, and an agreement between the seller and purchaser of real estate to defraud a lender by setting a higher than actual value on a piece of property. Some would say that it is the parties' agreement and not the concern of the mediator. However, most professionals agree that a mediator faced with such a dilemma can first attempt to explain to the parties that they are reaching what appears to be an illegal contract and urge them to reconsider their agreement. If they refuse, then the neutral should not participate in the settlement process. He can withdraw from the mediation at this point, leaving the door open for further mediation if the parties agree.

Appropriate Parties and Unrepresented Interests

What should a mediator do if she believes that the parties attending the mediation session are not in fact the parties who properly should be present, e.g., when parents appear at the session when their children should be there, or when a party is represented by someone who lacks the authority to commit to an agreement? Take the case of a community dispute over the behavior of someone's 12-year-old child. Should the child be present? the parent? both? Can the parent make an agreement that is binding on the child? The mediator can ask that the absent party join the session at a reconvened time. If that is not feasible, the mediator can proceed based on the premise that even nonparties can benefit from the mediation and convey the information to the real parties. Whether or not to proceed should be left to the discretion of the parties or their representatives who are present, since it is their dispute and their process.

Similar to the foregoing is the issue of unrepresented parties whose interests may be affected by the mediation. Examples are the aged, infants, and other potentially disenfranchised groups. The mediator may suggest that those interests be represented by an additional person invited to the mediation. Some say the mediator is responsible to protect those interests. However, to do so may adversely affect the mediator's neutrality. Most would agree that the mediation should proceed, even if unrepresented parties are not present, with an attempt to bring their needs before those who are present and suggest that they be considered in any agreement.

Which people should be at the table and who should represent whom. . . .
Mediators debate vigorously among themselves about the extent of their

responsibility to bring such unrepresented constituencies to the bargaining table. There is consensus, however, that if groups believe they have been excluded unfairly, their lack of participation will undercut any agreements reached in their absence.[34]

Power Imbalances

A serious power imbalance between the disputants can create an ethical issue for the mediator. Should a mediation proceed where there is a significant power imbalance between the parties? This will depend on the skill and subjective judgment of the mediator. Can the parties benefit from participation in the process even with the power imbalance? Is the imbalance even an issue? Can the mediator rectify the imbalance? Should the mediator attempt to balance out the power distribution?

A mediator can use the private setting of a caucus to try to overcome the effects of one party's intimidation or lack of assertiveness.

> In extreme cases, however, there are legitimate concerns about whether it is useful — or even appropriate — to attempt to mediate when resources, knowledge, or political power clearly is unequal (in a dispute between a car owner and General Motors, for example). In these circumstances, two questions need to be answered: whether it is possible to educate the less savvy parties about the process . . . and whether some access to expertise (legal or technical advice, for example) can be furnished to those who do not have it otherwise available. . . . The difficulty with declining to mediate in a situation of power imbalances is that mediation may be at least as well suited to the task as are any other available alternatives.[35]

Language

How does a mediator deal with non-English speaking disputants? Should there be an official interpreter or should one utilize the family member or friend that the party often brings? Generally, a non-official interpreter will not translate directly and may intersperse her own personal feelings and interpretations. This greatly complicates communication, which is an essential element of the process. The interpreter can be instructed to interpret precisely what is said and not to editorialize; but because the interpreter is not a trained professional, this instruction may

---

34. Singer, *supra* note 6, at 132-133.
35. *Id.* at 177.

have to be repeated throughout the mediation. However, if it is the only way to proceed, and the parties desire, then mediation should proceed.

Disclosure of Criminal Activity

What should a mediator do if a crime is disclosed during the mediation session? If it is a past crime, there is no requirement to disclose it. While the mediator may have been told of an act that appears to be a crime, it is not the role of the mediator to sit as judge and jury to determine if there was actually a crime committed. If it is a declaration that the party will commit a future crime, and the mediator is an attorney, she must report it under the attorney's Code of Professional Responsibility. Unless the mediator is an attorney or is operating under a similar code that requires disclosure, then it is a matter of conscience for the individual mediator.

Summary

Mediation is a dispute resolution process that involves the intervention of a third-party neutral to facilitate the parties' settlement negotiations. It is a flexible process and may take many forms. There are, however, certain invariables. The mediator must be neutral and must be knowledgeable and skilled in the mediation process. The parties should, at a minimum, be amenable to hearing about the process and, optimally, be prepared to negotiate to resolution.

The varied forms presented here include community mediation, business or commercial mediation, single-text mediation, and co-mediation. The process, to some degree, is as diverse as those who use it and those who serve as neutrals. The major difference among the various forms of mediation is the degree of the neutral's participation in formulating an agreement — from a neutral who only facilitates communication to one who makes suggestions and urges resolution.

The mediation process can be broken into three general steps. The first is the mediator introduction including explanation of the process, confidentiality, ground rules, and other orientation issues. The second step is facilitated negotiation, which includes the parties' initial statements, other fact gathering, brainstorming, reality testing, and determining the parties' real interests and in what manner they overlap.

Finally, there is a closing, in which the parties reach and affirm an agreement, in whole or in part, or suspend the mediation.

A competent mediator must possess excellent facilitative and interpersonal skills. The former include well-developed, nonjudgmental communication skills enhanced by active listening and the ability to be affirming of a person's emotional communications. Among the interpersonal skills the mediator must have are the ability to guide without forcing, to aid in creative thinking, to provide face-saving techniques and a safe environment, and to keep the process moving and the parties focused.

Neutrality is an important aspect of mediation. The mediator must give the appearance of lack of bias and must avoid a conflict of interest. While maintaining neutrality, a mediator may also have to consider power imbalances between the parties, whether it is appropriate to intervene in the power picture, and whether that intervention adversely affects neutrality.

Mediation is being applied in a growing number of diverse subject areas. Mediation originated in the community-based programs and continues to provide services in that area. Peer mediation is being used in public and parochial schools as well as colleges and universities. The court systems use mediation in criminal victim-offender programs, in civil matters including a significant emphasis on family mediation, and in administrative law matters. In the commercial area, mediation is used for labor-management disputes, construction disputes, environmental disputes, and general business conflicts. Many of these areas where mediation has been put to good use have grown out of contracts authorizing use of the mediation process. Particularly unique models of mediation are utilized in both international mediation and processes originating out of indigenous communities.

Ethical considerations must be closely monitored. The ABA, AAA, and SPIDR have developed joint standards of conduct for mediators which include issues of party self-determination, impartiality of the mediator, confidentiality of the process (with limitations), avoidance of conflicts of interest, and mediator competence.

In addition, mediators must avoid illegal settlement agreements, ensure the appropriate parties are at the mediation table, and deal with power imbalances between the parties.

Sensitivity to cultural as well as linguistic diversity can be important in some mediations.

EXERCISES

1. Research the court-annexed mediation available in your state or county. List the types of courts where it is used. Is it mandated in any of those courts? Who serves as mediator? Do they use individual mediators or a panel?

2. List the private providers of mediation services in your area. Who serves as mediator? What is the cost? What types of conflicts do they mediate? Do they use individual mediators or a panel?

3. Observe a mediation and report on the skills the mediator used, including presentation of the opening statement. Describe the conflict and the results of the mediation.

4. Research your state's Rules of Professional Conduct and Ethics Opinions for attorneys and determine the following:

    a. Can attorneys serve as mediators and then prepare the mediated agreement?
    b. Can attorneys offer mediation services out of their law offices?
    c. Have any other ethical issues regarding mediation come before the Ethics Committee in your state and, if so, what was the issue and the outcome?

5. Are there any educational or training requirements for individuals doing court-annexed (or court-referred) mediation? If so, what are they?

6. If you know anyone who has participated in a mediation, interview them about how they view and evaluate the process and the results.

7. Prepare a written opening statement and then present it to the class.

8. Determine where paralegals can and do serve as mediators in your area. Are they compensated?

9. Do a bias inventory of yourself. What groups or types of individuals do you have difficulty dealing with? How would you maintain your neutrality if mediating with such an individual or group representative?

Mediation Role Plays

Neighborhood Dispute (four parties)

John and Jossie Tarnet are a married couple who are in their mid-40s, and one year ago they moved into a downtown location of a desirable urban community. The homes are newer, but the lots relatively small (50- to 75-feet wide), making some contact with neighbors unavoidable. Both John and Jossie are professionals, but enjoy caring for their home and the yard. They have two adult children living with them, a 21-year-old son named Sigi and a 23-year-old daughter named Mary. Both children work and attend college. On one side of the Tarnets live Jake and Eustice Johnson, an older couple who have been in the neighborhood a long time and who are friendly with the Tarnets. There is an old fence between the properties, but it is not of much use.

The properties are not sunny due to the presence of numerous trees. The older couple has started a vegetable garden in the front yard, because there is absolutely no sun in the small rear yard. This has greatly distressed the Tarnets. They believe it is an inappropriate use of the front yard and has an adverse affect on the appearance of the neighborhood, which generally consists of small, well-manicured lawns. One day, the Tarnet's dog was unattended in the yard and wandered over to the neighbors' garden and used it as her bathroom. The neighbors did not see this, but saw the results and believed it to be the work of the Tarnet's dog. Several weeks later, coming home late one night and very tired from a full day at work and school, Mary turned too widely into the driveway and ended up in the Johnson's vegetable garden, further damaging it. The next day she went over to apologize to the Johnsons, but they refused to listen to her or anyone from the Tarnet household because they had come to believe that the Tarnet family is actively sabotaging their garden.

One Saturday morning at about 8:30, the Tarnets were out doing their yard work and using a gas-powered leaf blower to blow the driveway clean of grass clippings. Suddenly, the police showed up and issued a summons for disturbing the peace and violating the local noise ordinance. The Tarnets surmised that the Johnsons had called the police and reported them. They had thought the misunderstanding would eventually resolve itself; instead it seemed to be escalating. Mrs. Tarnet had heard about a community mediation center and decided to give this new thing a try. She called the center and asked them to intervene.

The Center wrote a letter to both parties, scheduling a meeting on a weeknight to inform them about the process and how the community center works. Both couples arrive and view the introductory videotape and agree to meet with you, the mediator.

Women in College

The college newspaper contained a large drawing of several very sexy semi-nude women wrestling with each other. Under it was the caption, "All the women are fighting for DXE men." It was intended to catch the eye of males who might be interested in pledging for DXE, a men's social fraternity that was seeking new members. In the same issue was an article by one of the male students on the editorial staff, Rock Tames, raging against the concept of "date rape," arguing that in his opinion, there was no such thing. This was in response to an announcement of a date rape seminar in the previous week's publication.

A number of women on campus were outraged by both the drawing and the article and brought the material to several feminist faculty members on campus. The Women's Center had an emergency meeting to discuss the problem. Before the meeting, the president of DXE was contacted to see if he would issue a public apology for the drawing, which the women believed denigrated women and reduced them to sex symbols. He refused to issue an apology, saying it was all done in good fun and that the women were making a big deal out of nothing. The newspaper was also approached and a retraction of the article requested, to no avail. Dr. Janice Wooster brought to the meeting a draft of a letter she wanted to have published in the school paper in response to both the ad and the article, which she claimed indicated strongly felt anti-female sympathies on campus. Her letter was extremely anti-male and strongly worded and the other members said that if it was to officially come from the Women's Center, it had to be toned down and made to sound more rational. They worked on it together and came up with a final draft. When submitted, the school paper refused to print it.

Outraged, representatives of the Women's Center approached the Dean of Students, who called a public meeting of the editorial staff of the newspaper, the students, and faculty from the Women's Center and any other interested parties, including staff. Much to the Dean's surprise, nearly 250 people showed up at the meeting, which quickly turned into such a free-for-all that security had to be called to disband the meeting. The Dean forbade the newspaper to print anything on the subject until the matter was resolved. He did not have the authority to do so, but the paper complied. However, posters started to show up around campus and in the residence halls, calling the Women's Center members "dykey bitches" and the newspaper's staff "chauvinist rapists."

A sociology professor who teaches conflict resolution approached the Dean and suggested that this matter be brought before the newly formed peer mediation center on campus. She reminded the Dean that the Center was comprised of students who had been trained in mediation and who could sit as neutrals to help the parties try to resolve their differences. The Dean was skeptical, but took the idea to the Provost, who by this time was decidedly unhappy about the lack of progress in resolving this issue. The matter had leaked to the outside press and it was creating negative publicity for the college. The Provost indicated that she thought mediation a good idea, so long as there was a panel of mediators, instead of a single mediator, and so long as the administration was represented at the mediation.

A letter was sent from the Office of the President inviting two representatives from the Women's Center and two representatives from the editorial staff to attend the mediation session. The young man who wrote the article about date rape was also invited. Three mediators were chosen: one white female, one black male, and one white male. They were chosen for their abilities as well as to ensure a diverse gender and ethnic mix. A Hispanic female from the President's office also was to attend to represent the administration. The press found out about the mediation and wanted to attend, but access was denied.

You are one of the panel of mediators. It is important to meet with the other mediators to determine who will make the opening statement and how the mediation should progress. You are concerned about the volatility of this issue.

Corporate Legal Department

Lanex Corporation has an in-house corporate legal department consisting of two secretaries, four paralegals, and three attorneys. There has been a great deal of unrest in the department since the addition of the most recently hired attorney, Shirley Downs. Finally, one of the secretaries, Tammy Whine, filed a personnel grievance with the union indicating that Ms. Downs was treating her unfairly, giving her an unrealistic amount of work, and expecting her to work during breaks and after working hours. Ms. Downs responded that the allegations were untrue and that Ms. Whine was underproducing. Ms. Downs had been hired to replace the former general counsel and to make the department more productive; that was what she was trying to do.

One of the paralegals, Alice Tokla, has put in for a transfer to the contracts department. There is an opening there, but her skills are probably put to better use in the legal department. The company wants to know why she is seeking the transfer — more particularly, whether it is due to the personnel problems in legal.

One of the problems is that the former general counsel was a very likeable guy. However, he had an alcohol problem that was diminishing his ability to work productively. He had attended the Alcoholics Anonymous unit in the company and improved for a while, but he later regressed and refused help. However, none of the people in legal know of his problem, only that he was let go and replaced by Ms. Downs. The entire department was very unhappy with his departure.

Company policy is going to require total computerization of the legal department within three months. Some people, particularly Ms. Whine, are resisting. Almost everyone else is looking forward to it. In addition to providing word processing and spreadsheet programs, the company will subscribe to either LEXIS or WESTLAW, which will be a great boon to the paralegals.

In addition to the foregoing, the company is probably going to be bought out by Intex and that may create more problems. Rumors are running wild. Will legal be replaced by Intex's legal department? Will certain corporate sections have to move to Intex's location over 150 miles away? Are their jobs secure? Is Shirley Downs really a spy for Intex? All of the employees' free time is spent discussing these and other scenarios. Everyone is on edge.

The union has brought the grievance to corporate personnel. Both have agreed to have a mediator from the ombuds office meet informally with all individuals in the legal department to gather information and then sit down with Ms. Downs and Ms. Whine to help them work out their differences if possible.

Arbitration

Introduction

Private and Court-Annexed Arbitration

How Do Disputants Come to Arbitration?

Binding and Nonbinding Arbitration

Mandatory or Voluntary Arbitration

Applications
    Labor Relations
    Commercial Arbitration
    Court-Annexed Arbitration
    Consumer Disputes
    Other Applications

Understanding the Process
    Preparation
    Procedure
    Final-Offer Arbitration
    Attorney and Paralegal Roles

The Arbitrator's Role

Ethics

Summary

Exercises

Introduction

> Arbitration, or private decisionmaking, has been used in the United States since its early commercial history. . . . Although its popularity has declined somewhat in favor of newer forms of dispute resolution, which permit the parties to retain some control over the outcome, arbitration still is used predominantly in businesses desiring private, binding decisions by third-party neutrals.[1]

Arbitration is adjudicatory in nature and is most like litigation. A third-party neutral, or panel of neutrals, hears each disputant's presentation of his or her case, including sworn testimony, documentary evidence, and physical evidence. Frequently, parties are represented by counsel. At the end of the presentations, the neutral makes an award, i.e., decides the case in favor of one party or the other. While the process can be less formal than the courtroom and the arbitrators are not always bound by the rules of evidence or precedent, arbitration is more formal than negotiation or mediation and has its own procedural and substantive rules. It has a long and distinguished history in some areas, such as commercial arbitration and labor disputes. "George Washington, for example, included a provision in his will calling for arbitration of any conflict that might arise over the interpretation of his will and the distribution of his estate."[2]

Arbitration can occur privately or through the court system; the mandate to arbitrate can come from a statute, a court rule, a contract between the disputants, or custom; and the arbitration can be binding or nonbinding, mandatory or voluntary. Practically any combination of these is possible. For example, one can have private, binding, contractually based arbitration, or one can have court-annexed, nonbinding, statutory based arbitration.

Arbitration will continue to grow as a dispute resolution process because (1) it is private and aids in avoiding publicity; (2) it offers more rapid resolution of conflicts that otherwise would be delayed by crowded court dockets; and (3) it offers the parties some degree of autonomy through the selection of an arbitrator.

---

1. Linda R. Singer, Settling Disputes: Conflict Resolution in Business, Families, and The Legal System 27 (2d ed. 1994).
2. Susan M. Leeson & Bryan M. Johnston, Ending It: Dispute Resolution in America 48 (1988).

Private and Court-Annexed Arbitration

Private arbitration is a process chosen by the parties outside of the court system. They choose an arbitrator(s) or go through one of the private providers of arbitration services, such as the American Arbitration Association. The parties' dispute and its resolution through the award of the arbitrator is never made part of any public record unless they so desire or it is the custom of their field. The parties themselves pay for the services of the arbitrator.

Court-annexed arbitration takes place in the courthouse by arbitrators provided by the court system and under court authority. The parties have less control over the process, as they do not choose the arbitrators or the arbitration rules to be followed. However, since the parties have little choice in this process, the award is nonbinding. This process does not cost the parties anything unless they appeal it.

How Do Disputants Come to Arbitration?

The most common source of arbitration cases is a contractual agreement. Parties enter into a business contract that provides that if there is a dispute over the contract or the relationship it creates, that dispute will be arbitrated. Some such clauses are general and state simply that "[A]ny difference or dispute arising under this contract will be resolved through arbitration. . . ." Other clauses specifically delineate what matters can be arbitrated.[3] They can further specify controls, such as what rules govern, who serves as arbitrator, and the number of arbitrators. Contract-based arbitration is private.

If the parties do not have a contractual relationship requiring them to arbitrate, they can still agree to use the process. Such arrangements are considered voluntary and usually provide for binding arbitration, which means that the parties are bound by the award of the arbitrator and can only appeal it in specified legal contexts.[4]

---

3. *Id.* at 50.

4. For a list of grounds for setting aside an arbitration award by the court, see *infra* at pages 99-109.

Throughout the country, statutory authority and court rules are emerging that require arbitration, particularly in certain classes of cases that are within the court system. An example is the requirement that all cases in trial court involving automobile property damage in excess of $10,000 must go to arbitration. This type of arbitration is court-annexed and nonbinding.

The labor field is governed by both custom and contract and it relies extensively on private, binding arbitration for resolution of disputes. Examples of labor issues frequently arbitrated include private employee matters, public employee salaries, and sports figures' salaries.

Binding and Nonbinding Arbitration

"Binding arbitration" means that the arbitrator's award is final and generally not appealable. It is found in the private sector and is entered into by agreement or custom. The arbitrator's authority in binding arbitration comes from the terms of the contract or agreement that brings the parties to the arbitration forum and his award is governed by that same contract. The courts traditionally have honored binding arbitration awards and rarely overturned them, doing so on very limited grounds.

Nonbinding arbitration, on the other hand, is mandated by the court or is court-annexed. In this type of dispute resolution, the parties are notified, after initial pleadings are filed with the court, to appear before an arbitrator to present their case. At the end of this hearing, the arbitrator makes an award. If the parties are satisfied with the arbitrator's award, it becomes a judgment after a specified period of time. If either party is dissatisfied and so notifies the court within that specified time, there is a trial de novo[5] of the matter. There is usually a penalty for requesting a trial de novo, such as payment of a fee, or a penalty if one is not more successful in court than they were in arbitration. One must also consider the additional time and cost involved in continuing through the judicial process.

It concerns some consumer advocates that nonbinding arbitration might be seen as just an additional step litigants have to take before getting to court, and in this respect have a chilling effect on a party's interest in litigating. However, others point out that the dispute is processed more quickly in arbitration and that benefits the party's. One of the

5. Literally, "from the beginning," as if the arbitration had not taken place.

drawbacks of nonbinding arbitration is that some seasoned litigants or their representatives take it less seriously than a court hearing and therefore prepare less for the arbitration and appear to be just "going through the motions."

Mandatory or Voluntary Arbitration

Whether arbitration is mandatory or voluntary determines whether the parties are required to participate in arbitration or choose to do so. Generally court-ordered or court-annexed arbitration, based in statute or court rules, is mandatory arbitration, i.e., the parties do not have a choice. Contractual arbitration or that arising out of custom is considered voluntary, since it arises out of the initial voluntary act of entering into a contract. Likewise, if parties find themselves in a dispute and choose private arbitration, their process is considered voluntary.

To summarize the foregoing, a dispute over a contract that contains an arbitration clause will proceed to private, binding arbitration, which is voluntary and governed by the contract. A matter in which a complaint has been filed in court, which falls under the statute requiring arbitration, will be arbitrated in the courthouse and the arbitration is considered mandatory and nonbinding. It can generally be said that if arbitration is mandatory or court-annexed, it is nonbinding; and if it is voluntary and private, it is binding. Note, however, some of the exceptions that follow.

Applications

Labor Relations

Labor arbitration is considered voluntary and binding.

Most states . . . have enacted statutes requiring arbitration of labor-management disputes, particularly those involving public sector employees such as teachers, police, and firefighters. Today over 90 percent of all collective bargaining agreements specify arbitration for the resolution of disputes. . . .

Arbitration in the labor-management context can take two forms.

One is called interest arbitration, which occurs when the parties have reached impasse in the collective bargaining process. If they cannot agree to the terms of a contract through negotiation or mediation, an arbitrator can be called in to declare what the rights of the respective parties will be under the proposed contract. The second form is called grievance arbitration. It occurs when a dispute arises under an existing contract and the parties cannot agree about the meaning or significance of the terms.[6]

When the labor dispute is one involving public service employees such as fire fighters or the police, the form of arbitration is compulsory, binding, and interest-based, as opposed to voluntary, nonbinding, and grievance-based. In disputes involving professional sports figures, both salary and grievance arbitration are used, and "final offer" arbitration (see page 107) is particularly favored.

Commercial Arbitration

Commercial arbitration occurs on an international level, on a national level, and on the local level. "The International Chamber of Commerce, the American Arbitration Association, and the State of Hawaii are among those competing for the international commercial dispute resolution business."[7] It is usually contract-based and business-oriented.

Arbitration has broad applicability in business. Where parties want to submit their dispute to an expert in their own business, they generally will use arbitration; where there is a continuing relationship between parties which they can't afford to rupture, they will provide for arbitration to decide their disputes; where there is a practical need for a prompt and final decision, businesspeople often arbitrate.[8]

Commercial arbitration is binding.

Court-Annexed Arbitration

This is a growing area of practice. It is usually the creature of statute or court rule, both of which can

establish criteria that identify cases eligible for arbitration. Disputants whose cases fit these criteria must participate in arbitration as a prerequisite to trial. In contrast, commercial arbitration has traditionally been

6. Leeson & Johnston, *supra* note 2, at 49.
7. *Id.* at 49.
8. Robert Coulson, How to Stay Out of Court 145 (1985).

available as an option for litigants who wished to escape the civil trial track. A secondary distinction between commercial arbitration and CAA [court-annexed arbitration] is that CAA is mandatory but nonbinding; all arbitration decisions may be appealed. On the other hand, commercial arbitration, entered into voluntarily, is binding upon the parties to a dispute.[9]

Court-annexed arbitration programs vary within each jurisdiction, as well as from state to state. "The principal procedural dimension that distinguishes CAA programs [from one another] appears to be whether the program's procedural rules are geared to increase the speed of civil dispute resolution. Some programs place strict time limits on all aspects of pre- and post-hearing procedures while others are much more permissive[10]." For example, parties to a CAA may have a 30-day time period within which to appeal the award and request a trial de novo.

[E]ach of the state court-annexed arbitration programs contains some provision for reconsideration of the arbitration decision. Any party may appeal the decision by requesting a trial de novo. The state restrictions on re-entry into the civil litigation track vary primarily in terms of time limits for filing an appeal and disincentives to appealing the arbitration decision. These disincentives most commonly come in the form of fees to appeal and potential liability for costs of the arbitration if the appellant does not appeal and potential liability for costs of the arbitration if the appellant does not improve his or her position at trial. They are designed to ensure . . . participation in the arbitration process and to encourage the conclusion of the litigation. Without disincentives to appeal, CAA could be viewed by attorneys and litigants as simply another discovery device rather than as a viable technique for ending the dispute.[11]

Arbitration is also a part of the federal judicial system.

Arbitration is expected in civil actions [federal] in which the relief sought involves only monetary damages of $100,000 or less, exclusive of interest and legal expenses. The district courts are to presume that civil actions fall within the boundaries of this program unless counsel certifies otherwise. Procedural rules established by legislation include the requirements that:

- hearings take place within 180 days of the answer to the complaint;
- trial de novo is guaranteed;

9. John P. McIver & Susan Keilitz, Court-Annexed Arbitration: An Introduction, 13 Just. Sys. 123 (1991).

10. *Id.* at 127.

11. McIver & Keilitz, *supra* note 8, at 127.

- a request for trial de novo must be filed within 30 days of the filing of the arbitration award;
- a trial de novo case must be restored to the court docket as if it had not been arbitrated;
- arbitration evidence and results are sealed to district court judge until the conclusion of the trial de novo.[12]

Consumer Disputes

Consumer arbitration covers a wide variety of disputes between consumers and providers, such as the automobile industry, the insurance industry, or the securities industry. The Better Business Bureau is at the forefront of consumer arbitration. One area of consumer arbitration — disputes over new cars that are found unsatisfactory by the consumer — has been expanded through the enactment of "lemon laws." These

entitle consumers to a rebate or a new car if they have recurring complaints during the warranty period [and they] require consumers to go to an arbitration program if it meets certain prescribed standards, before suing the manufacturer. Some states, including Conn., Mass., and Maryland, have responded by setting up their own mediation and arbitration programs. In Connecticut, arbitration panels use an independent expert to advise them on technical issues in order to balance the manufacturers' technical advantage.[13]

Other consumer disputes may reach arbitration through contract.

Stockbrokers, automobile manufacturers, moving companies, law firms and health care organizations are examples of groups that commonly include arbitration clauses in their agreements with clients. Likewise, many insurance companies and their policyholders rely on arbitration to resolve uninsured motorist, extent of coverage, and other claims.[14]

Builders of new homes frequently provide purchasers certain warranties and include arbitration as a remedy for breach therof.

12. *Id.* at 131-132.
13. Singer, *supra* note 1, at 89-90.
14. Leeson & Johnston, *supra* note 2, at 49.

Other Applications

Many state environmental agencies and the federal Environmental Protection Agency (EPA) utilize the arbitration process. "Binding arbitration is available in EPA disputes involving less than $500,000."[15] Patent, copyright, and trademark disputes are also submitted to arbitration.

Understanding the Process

Preparation

Preparing for arbitration is like preparing for litigation. Discovery should be complete, evidence must be in order, witnesses should be prepared for testimony, and the attorney must have a thorough knowledge of the facts, the underlying contract, if any, and any applicable law. The paralegal's role in preparing for arbitration — preparing the file, doing factual and legal research, and preparing witnesses — is also the same as in preparing for litigation. It is extremely frustrating for the arbitrator, or one's adversary, to be faced with an unprepared attorney. It shows a lack of respect for the process and may be construed as an attempt to use the arbitration proceeding as a discovery tool or an opportunity to delay.

In some private arbitrations, there is occasionally an exchange of preliminary "pleadings," such as a Demand for Arbitration and an Answer and possible counterclaim. The documents are in written form and submitted to the sponsoring agency as well as to the opposing parties; they are brief in nature. The demand, for example, includes an outline of the dispute and the amount of damages or other remedy sought.

Either the parties will have chosen the arbitrator from a list supplied to them or, if they are unable to agree, the sponsoring agency will have chosen an arbitrator for them. There may have been a preliminary hearing to establish discovery deadlines and schedule hearings and other preparatory matters. The parties may also have exchanged information, like witness lists.

---

15. Singer, *supra* note 1, at 139.

Procedure

While each arbitration is unique, a basic format is followed. The hearing does not take place in a courtroom, but in a "hearing" room. The arbitrator (or arbitrators) introduces herself and determines the names of all present and the role they play. Anyone who is going to testify is sworn in by the arbitrator. If necessary, the arbitration process is explained so that the participants know what to expect. In some instances, the hearing is recorded by a court reporter, although usually the arbitrator maintains a record of the hearing. The record usually includes the names and addresses of witnesses and copies of all documentary evidence submitted. All evidence is marked as in a trial.

The attorneys, or the parties themselves, can make opening statements, which include a summary of their side of the dispute. This is followed by the testimony of witnesses and the introduction of documentary and other physical evidence. The party demanding the arbitration presents his case first, followed by the opposing party. Each side has the opportunity to cross-examine and provide rebuttal testimony as in a trial. While the hearing is not bound by the rules of evidence, such rules can be used as a guidepost. Upon completion of the presentation of each side's case, the attorneys or parties are given the opportunity to make closing arguments. The arbitrator may request that the attorneys brief — i.e., prepare a detailed, written argument — a particular legal issue. Once all factual and legal issues are presented, the hearing is closed, after which the arbitrator has a stipulated period of time in which to render an award. Sometimes a party will request that a hearing be reopened to consider new evidence.

Arbitrations can be very brief — as short as one hour — or can take an extended period of time. The arbitrator can be an attorney, or an expert in the field that is the subject matter of the dispute. In some instances, the disputing parties retain control over the process and over the standards used in resolving the dispute.[16] "Parties who have not agreed beforehand to submit their dispute to arbitration can elect the process after a dispute arises."[17] In private arbitration, the arbitrator's fee is paid by the parties.

There are various providers of private dispute resolution services. They include the American Arbitration Association, the Federal Mediation and Conciliation Service, and the National Academy of Arbitrators.

---

16. Leeson & Johnston, *supra* note 2, at 47.
17. *Id.* at 50.

Final-Offer Arbitration

Some states require final-offer or last-offer arbitration. It is a popular vehicle in professional sports salary negotiations.

> With minor modifications, it works as follows. Negotiations are divided into two phases. In Phase 1 the parties bargain directly with or without the aid of an intervenor (mediator). If the parties agree, there is no second phase. If the parties disagree, the negotiations enter Phase 2, at which point the arbitrator enters the scene. In most states the arbitrator does not obtain guidance or information from the mediator present in Phase 1. The arbitrator determines the facts and then demands from each party a sealed final offer. These final offers are submitted essentially simultaneously, and the arbitrator must then, by law, select one of these two final offers; no in-between compromises are permissible, and the selected final offer becomes binding on both sides. . . . [F]inal offer arbitration is quite effective in persuading parties to settle without an imposed arbitrated solution.[18]

The theory supporting the use of final-offer arbitration is that the parties will be reasonable in their final offer, believing that the arbitrator will choose the most reasonable offer under the circumstances.

Attorney and Paralegal Roles

"Lawyers play three important roles in voluntary arbitration. First, they negotiate and draft contracts. Second, they represent parties in arbitration. Third, they serve as arbitrators."[19] The same is true of paralegals. First, they draft contracts, review contracts, and develop form banks that contain dispute resolution clauses for inclusion in contracts, orders, and agreements. Second, they assist in preparing the matter for arbitration. Third, the paralegal can attend the hearing with the attorney and take notes, provide documents, and in general assist the attorney. Finally, arbitrators need not be attorneys. If a paralegal has a field of specialization and a professional history in that field, she can combine arbitration training with that specialization and serve as an arbitrator.

---

18. Howard Raiffa, The Art & Science of Negotiation 110-111 (1982).
19. Leeson & Johnston, *supra* note 2, at 53.

The Arbitrator's Role

"The arbitrator or arbitration panel is responsible for the conduct of the hearing. In addition to the general tasks of convening the session and directing the flow of the procedure, the arbitrator has the task of maintaining control over the disputants and their representatives."[20] "A good arbitrator should be decisive, comfortable running a hearing, capable of distinguishing facts from opinions, and, where required, able to write reasoned decisions."[21]

Someone who is an experienced mediator and who enjoys the mediation process may have difficulty serving as an arbitrator because the role is so different. The mediator is a facilitator who brings the parties to their own agreement. The arbitrator hears evidence and decides who will win and who will lose the case, based upon the contract and the law.

The mandatory qualifications of arbitrators vary within jurisdictions and within state programs. For example, in some programs — Arizona, Colorado, and Missouri, among others — lay arbitrators are permitted. Other programs require attorney arbitrators. Still others require attorney arbitrators to have a minimum number of professional years of experience. On the other hand, the field of labor/management arbitration does not use attorney arbitrators at all.

Another arbitrator qualification is knowledge of the subject matter and minimum number of years of experience in that field, such as construction, real estate, or labor relations. There are opportunities to serve as a voluntary arbitrator (Better Business Bureau) as well as opportunities for compensated service (American Arbitration Association).

Ethics

The arbitrator is responsible for maintaining the integrity and fairness of the arbitration hearing. This means that the arbitrator must actively demonstrate fairness toward the parties and avoid any hint of bias. It further requires that an arbitrator disclose any potential conflict of interest and avoid any future conflict of interest. For example, an arbitrator should have no financial or personal dealings with either of the parties.

20. *Id.* at 50.
21. Singer, *supra* note 1, at 173.

An arbitrator must decide the case within the confines of the contract or the agreement that brought the matter to arbitration, and not exceed that authority. Further, the process should be conducted diligently and without undue delay. The arbitrator must also maintain the confidentiality of the process.

Arbitration awards are generally upheld and enforced when appealed to the court. But courts do have limited power to vacate an arbitration award, granted under the United States Arbitration Act, 9 U.S.C. §§1-14 (1925). Section 10 of the Act states:

In either of the following cases in the United States[, the] court in and for the district wherein the award was made may make an order vacating the award upon the application of any party to the arbitration —

    (a) Where the award was procured by corruption, fraud, or undue means.

    (b) Where there was evident partiality or corruption in the arbitrators, or either of them.

    (c) Where the arbitrators were guilty of misconduct in refusing to postpone the hearing, upon sufficient cause shown, or in refusing to hear evidence pertinent and material to the controversy; or of any other misbehavior by which the rights of any party have been prejudged.

    (d) Where the arbitrators exceeded their powers, or so imperfectly executed them that a mutual, final and definite award upon the subject matter submitted was not made.

    (e) Where an award is vacated and the time within which the agreement required the award to be made has not expired the court may, in its discretion, direct a rehearing by the arbitrators.[22]

Sometimes the court's intervention is sought by a party at the commencement of the arbitration, over the issue of whether a particular contract or a particular issue is subject to arbitration (arbitrability issues). While an arbitrator may decide in favor of or against arbitrability, that decision is considered a matter of law and is reviewable by the courts. Alternatively, if one of the parties originally brings the matter before the court, without proceeding in arbitration, the courts can order the arbitration of a matter that is the subject of an agreement to arbitrate. Courts generally resolve arbitrability issues in favor of arbitration.[23]

22. *Quoted in* Leeson & Johnston, *supra* note 2, at 72-73.
23. See, e.g., Moses M. Cone Memorial Hosp. v. Mercury Const. Corp., 460 U.S. 1, 24-25 (1983).

Is an arbitrator subject to "neutral liability"? "To date, arbitrators have been afforded fairly broad immunity from attack on their decisions. They have been held liable for their failure to decide a case once they have accepted it however."[24]

A final issue that has arisen within the past several years is the requirement by an employer that a new employee sign an employment contract that contains an arbitration clause. If the employee signs such a contract unaware of the arbitration clause, is she bound by it? The United States Supreme Court has found "yes."[25]

Summary

Arbitration is a dispute resolution process that uses a third-party to determine the outcome of a dispute; an arbitrator hears the case and makes an award. Arbitration is used extensively in the private sector and is expanding in court-annexed programs. Usually in the former, the process arises out of a contractual obligation and the award is binding, while in the latter, the court mandates arbitration in pending litigation and the award is not binding.

The fields most likely to seek private arbitration of disputes include labor, commerce, and consumer applications in the insurance, securities, and automobile industries, among others. Court-related arbitration can also be found at many levels within the federal system; for example, administrative agencies like the EPA are taking advantage of the benefits of arbitration. Court-annexed or lawsuit-related arbitration is usually mandated by statute or court rule.

The arbitration hearing itself is similar to a court hearing, but is less formal. The parties and/or their counsel should prepare as they would for a trial. The arbitrator hears opening statements and oral testimony, reviews documentary evidence, and permits oral argument before making an award. The paralegal can have a pivotal role in preparing for the arbitration, and can attend the hearing with the attorney.

A good arbitrator conducts an efficient and bias-free hearing, pursuant to either contract or statute, and makes a fair and independent award based upon the contract or the law. As part of her ethical responsibility, an arbitrator must avoid any conflict of interest and maintain confidentiality. The court will rarely overturn an arbitration award and

---

24. Singer, *supra* note 1, at 180.
25. Gilmer v. Interstate/Johnson Lane Corp., 500 U.S. 20 (1991).

limits its review to issues of corruption, fraud, undue influence, evident partiality, misconduct, and instances where the arbitrator exceeded her powers.

EXERCISES

1. Check the statutes of your state to determine if your state has adopted the Uniform Arbitration Act.

2. Is ambiguity in an arbitration award sufficient reason for setting it aside? Read *Steelworkers v. Enterprise Corp.*, 363 U.S. 593 (1960).

3. Can a court award counsel fees against a party that has failed to abide by a grievance-arbitration condition of a collective bargaining agreement? See *Bailey v. Bicknell Minerals, Inc.*, 819 F.2d 690 (7th Cir. 1987).

4. Are there any reporters that deal specifically with arbitration awards? If so, what are they?

5. Observe an arbitration proceeding and report on it to the class.

6. Where is court-annexed arbitration being used in your state?

7. Are there any private arbitration providers in your area? What credentials do they require of the arbitrators whose services they use?

8. Review the facts and the law in a fact pattern from your litigation class. Choose which side you want to represent and then do the legal research necessary to present the case. Choose a classmate to be your client and prepare them for the arbitration. You and the other attorney should jointly choose an arbitrator from among your classmates. Do a hearing and ask the arbitrator to provide a written award.

9. Do the same as in Exercise 8, but choose a panel of three arbitrators.

Other Forms of Dispute Resolution

Introduction

Adjudicative Processes
    Private Judging
    Med–Arb
    Final–Offer Arbitration

Court-Related Nonadjudicative Processes
    Mini-Trial
    Summary Jury Trial
    Focus Groups
    Neutral Expert Factfinding
    Early Settlement/Bar Paneling

Noncourt-Related Nonadjudicative Processes
    Ombudsperson
    Conciliation
    Facilitation

Summary

Exercises

Introduction

There are myriad forms of dispute resolution practiced in the United States today. Many follow the guidelines of one of the principal processes we have already considered;[1] others are a combination of the principal models to form a hybrid. For example, when disputants use med-arb, they initially try to resolve their dispute with the assistance of a mediator. If mediation does not result in an agreement, however, the process resorts to arbitration.

These diverse forms of dispute resolution can be classified as either adjudicative or nonadjudicative. In an adjudicative process, the neutral makes a decision or renders an award finally determining the issues presented. Alternatively, in a nonadjudicative process, the neutral serves as a facilitator/advisor rather than as a decisionmaker. Arbitration is an adjudicative form of dispute resolution and mediation is a nonadjudicative form.

In this chapter, forms of dispute resolution other than the three principal approaches will be defined, examples of them given, and their role in the overall scheme of dispute resolution discussed.

Adjudicative Processes

Adjudicative processes are those in which a decision by a neutral third party is imposed upon the disputants. The process can be voluntary or involuntary and the decision binding or nonbinding, depending on the particular process and, sometimes, the desire of the parties.

Private Judging

This is a private process in which the parties agree to employ a third-party neutral to hear and decide their case. The process is voluntary and binding, and it can be agreed upon when the parties enter into the contract that gives rise to their dispute or at any time thereafter. Private judging is usually chosen when the parties face the imminent prospect of a lengthy trial. In one instance, the parties and their counsel

---

1. Negotiation, mediation, or arbitration.

found themselves waiting too long to get a trial date, were concerned they would not get consecutive trial dates, and agreed to hire a retired judge to hear and decide their litigation. The process gives the parties control over the choice of a neutral as well as the scheduling of the hearing and the rules governing the process. This contributes to a more expedited proceeding with a neutral who has experience in the subject matter.

In some circumstances or jurisdictions, the choice to use a private judge is made entirely by the parties, without court intervention. In other jurisdictions, the court will refer certain cases to a private judge, or the parties can request a court referral to private judging.

> Some states (particularly California) provide for the parties selection of a "referee" who is paid by the parties and empowered by statute to enter a judgment having the finality, precedent value and appealability of a regular trial court decree. Other states (such as Florida and Texas) provide for the mandatory referral of court cases to private ADR providers, paid by the parties.[2]

> Under "rent-a-judge" statutes, parties file a joint petition with the court in which the case has been filed (known as the presiding court) requesting that the case be tried before a "rented" judge of the parties' selection. Typically, "rented" judges are retired judges or magistrates who know the law and the procedural requirements of a formal trial in that jurisdiction. If the court agrees, the case is assigned to the "rented" judge. The judge follows the jurisdiction's rules of evidence and procedure, and applies the jurisdiction's law in hearing the case. The judge submits findings of fact and conclusions of law to the presiding court. In some jurisdictions, the parties are given an opportunity to object to any findings or conclusions before the "rented" judge's opinion is submitted to the presiding judge and entered as the judgment of the court.
>
> After the judgment is entered, parties retain the same rights of enforcement and appeal they would have if the case were tried in the presiding court. The parties must pay the judge's salary. . . . Parties may be willing to share the cost of the judge because the procedure allows them to have their case tried quickly as opposed to having to wait their turn on the court docket, and they can select a judge with expertise in the subject matter of their dispute.[3]

There are criticisms of private judging. It is only available to those disputants who can afford to pay for it. Further, some say it removes the

---

2. Stephen B. Goldberg et al., Dispute Resolution: Negotiation, Mediation and Other Processes 291 (2d ed. 1992) (citations omitted).

3. Susan M. Leeson & Bryan M. Johnston, Ending It: Dispute Resolution in America 21-22 (1988).

pressure from the court to practice legal reform and drains off judicial resources, i.e., judges can retire from the public bench and "ascend" to the private bench. Finally, similar to the shortcomings of arbitration, because the decisions are private, they may not be a matter of public record and offer no precedent. However, some statutory schemes provide for both filing a private judgment and appealing a private award to an appellate court.[4]

How might the paralegal be involved in private judging? He may draft the original contract or agreement between the parties. All of the processes discussed herein can be provided for in a contract or agreement that initially brings the parties together. Such a contract can merely provide that if a dispute arises, the parties will seek to resolve it through a private judge (or med-arb, or mini-trial, or any one of these processes). However, the better approach is to provide as much detail as possible, including the service to be used or the name of the private judge, the rules to be followed (e.g., the rules of practice of a named jurisdiction), and whether the decision will be binding.

Alternatively, the paralegal who hears an attorney bemoaning the upcoming trial of an extremely complex, time-consuming matter may suggest that the parties consider a private judge who is familiar with this particular type of case. The paralegal can then research the various providers and submit the results of her research to the attorney for discussion with the client and the adversary. Once it has been agreed that a private judge will be hired, trial preparation will proceed as usual.

Med-Arb

This process is a combination of mediation and arbitration, but it is placed under adjudicative methods because if the mediation does not bring the parties to a full agreement then the matter is arbitrated, and arbitration is adjudicative in nature. What is problematic about this hybrid form is the continued use of the same neutral. The neutral has served in the mediation, hearing potentially confidential information from each party, and then if the parties fail to reach agreement in the mediation, the same neutral serves as an arbitrator, issuing a final and binding decision. Med-arb is not the same as the parties first participating in a mediation, which does not resolve their conflict, and thereafter submitting to arbitration with a different person or panel serving as arbitrator. In the latter situation, the parties have participated in two separate, successive

4. For a more in-depth discussion of the pros and cons of private judging, see Richard Chernick, Private Judging, 3 BNA Alternative Dispute Resolution Report 397 (1989).

processes. In the former, the processes are merged and the same third-party neutral utilized. While med-arb may save time because the parties do not have to present their case twice, it can adversely impact on the appearance of neutrality of the third party.

> The participants may, in some circumstances, agree or contract for the mediator to decide the matter if they are unable to do so. . . . Using the informal, consensual process of mediation with no evidentiary or procedural rules as the basis for an imposed decision does, however, create a considerable risk that the more clever or sophisticated participant may distort or manipulate the mediation in order to influence the mediator's opinion.
>
> A combined process of mediation followed by arbitration, all performed by one person, has been used with some success in labor conflicts. This "med-arb" approach may work best when the participants are of relatively equal bargaining experience and the efficiency of a combined procedure outweighs the inhibiting or strategic effect of the mediator's anticipated role change.[5]

Med-arb requires unusual skills on the part of the person who plays both roles. Mediators, after all, are retained to facilitate discussion and to help parties agree on their own solutions to problems. Arbitrators are retained to take evidence and to render a judgment following the parties' presentation of evidence. The dynamics of the two processes are substantially different: mediation strives to minimize the adversary nature of dispute, while arbitration works well within an adversary model. Because of its hybrid nature, med-arb seems most appropriate as a voluntary, private dispute resolution method with the parties having control over the choice of forum and the person or persons who serve as mediator-arbitrators.[6]

See Appendix C for an example.

Conceding that med-arb has an efficiency advantage over "pure" mediation followed by "pure" arbitration, it nonetheless has some disadvantages. Initially, disputing parties who know that the mediator also has decisional authority are likely to be less candid than they would be with a "pure" mediator about such matters as how they prioritize their interests and the least they will accept to resolve the dispute. They will be unwilling to be candid about these matters because they will fear that if no agreement is reached, the mediator turned arbitrator will use their disclosures against them. For example, a party's disclosure that it would settle for $5,000, rather than the $10,000 it has been demanding, might be used by

---

5. Jay Folberg & Alison Taylor, Mediation: A Comprehensive Guide to Resolving Conflicts Without Litigation 278 (1984).
6. Leeson & Johnston, *supra* note 3, at 151.

the mediator turned arbitrator to limit an award in favor of that party to $5,000. Hence, that party will not tell the mediator that, if necessary, it would settle for $5,000. Lacking that information the mediator may be unable to help the parties reach a settlement at $5,000. In sum, because the med-arb mediator is likely to have less information at his disposal than is the "pure" mediator, he is less likely to obtain mediated settlements.

If, on the other hand, the parties have been candid in the mediation process but no agreement is reached, the mediator turned arbitrator will possess information that he would not have acquired in a purely arbitral role. In the foregoing example, if the claimant disclosed his willingness to accept $5,000, the arbitrator, who is anxious to maintain the good will of both parties for future employment purposes, will find it difficult to ignore that fact in reaching a decision. Even if he does so and concludes independently that the claimant should receive only $5,000, the claimant will suspect that the arbitrator has improperly used information conveyed to him in mediation. Thus, the integrity of both mediation and arbitration is placed at risk when the same person serves as both mediator and arbitrator.[7]

In connection with med-arb, the paralegal might be asked to research the types of disputes that are being resolved through med-arb or the prevalence of its use in the pertinent jurisdiction or industry. He might develop a provision for a contract that provides for med-arb and defines its use and parameters. He might also suggest to the attorney that the parties consider using separate neutrals for each process, i.e., a mediator first, followed by a different arbitrator.

Final-Offer Arbitration

In this unique form of arbitration, the neutral must choose between the final offer of each disputant. In other words, the arbitrator cannot make a compromise decision but rather must pick one of the party's final offers. For example, assume that the salary negotiations for a baseball player have reached a stalemate and that the owners and the player go to final-offer arbitration. The player is seeking an annual salary of $500,000 and the owners are offering $200,000. While each might be willing to move from their position, closer to the other, they are afraid that if they do so the arbitrator may choose the salary midway between their respective offers. Therefore, if they stay at $200,000 and $500,000, an arbitrator might choose $350,000 as a compromise salary and make an award of that amount. But, if the owners, in an attempt at "good faith,"

---

7 Goldberg et al., *supra* note 2, at 226-227.

move up to $300,000 and the player does not change his offer, but remains at $500,000, the arbitrator might come in at $400,000. While this result will not necessarily occur, the possibility has a chilling effect on good-faith negotiations.

Final offer arbitration was devised to force the parties to make more realistic offers so that the arbitrator, who must choose between the two, will choose the most realistic offer. In the last example, the arbitrator would have to choose between $400,000 and $500,000 and, since the owners had made an effort toward compromise, might be likely to choose the $400,000 figure.

This type of process has arisen to resolve conflicts where the parties are negotiating prospectively (over a future contract, rather than a past breach of contract) but cannot effectively abandon the negotiation or the contract.

> Although arbitration is frequently used to resolve disputes about the interpretation or application of an existing contract, it is rarely used to resolve disputes about what the terms of a new contract should be. The reasons for the reluctance to use arbitration in this context are manifold. Parties who have an unresolvable dispute as to their rights under an existing contract must find some adjudicative means to determine those rights, but parties who have an unresolvable dispute concerning what their rights should be under a contract they are seeking to negotiate typically are under no such obligation. If they cannot agree, each is free to seek other parties with whom to negotiate. Hence, they tend to be reluctant to vest a third party with the power to decide what their rights against each other should be. This reluctance is typically overcome only when negotiating parties are required, for any of a number of reasons, to deal exclusively with each other and to reach agreement.[8]

Final-offer arbitration is also used in the area of public sector collective bargaining, for example, between municipal employee unions and the municipality.

> Final-offer arbitration is . . . frequently used to resolve "interest" disputes in public-sector employment. In baseball, however, arbitrators determine only the player's *salary* for one season; all of the other terms of employment are contained in the "Uniform Player's Contract" that is made part of the collective bargaining agreement. In contrast, public-sector "interest" arbitrators are frequently charged with determining a wide range of bargainable issues, all going to make up the terms of employment in the new agreement.

8. Goldberg et al., *supra* note 2, at 223-224.

In some states, the statutory scheme calls for each party to present to the arbitrators a "package" including a position on *all* the bargainable issues not yet agreed on. The arbitrators must then choose what they consider to be the most reasonable of the two "packages." In other states, in contrast, the arbitrators are allowed to consider each issue separately and to choose between the positions of the parties on an issue-by-issue basis. This variation enables them to develop their own compromise "package" by balancing the parties' positions on the various issues.[9]

A paralegal involved in final-offer arbitration might perform factual research about salaries of municipal employees in nearby towns, or towns with similar demographics to the town that the attorney represents. This information would aid the attorney in preparing for final-offer arbitration, because it would support the reasonableness of the client's offer.

Court-Related Nonadjudicative Processes

Mini-trial

Words sometimes catch the imagination and take on a life of their own, and so it is with the "mini-trial." This term was attached by a New York Times story to a formal settlement device created in 1977 in connection with a corporate dispute. [*Telecredit Inc., of Los Angeles v. TRW, Inc.*] It is not strictly speaking a trial at all, but a process that combines elements of adjudication with other processes such as negotiation and mediation.[10]

A mini-trial is particularly useful in resolving business disputes. It is a voluntary and private process of dispute resolution in which counsel for the parties are given the opportunity to present a summary of proofs and argument to an impartial third party who may have expertise in the area and who renders a decision based on the proofs presented. The presentation is made within an agreed-upon time frame and is made before top management representatives or individuals who have settlement authority. The parties may select the neutral, whose decision is not binding but, rather, is advisory and intended to assist the parties in reaching a mutually acceptable agreement. Sometimes the parties negotiate after the case is presented but before hearing the neutral's evaluation; sometimes they negotiate after.

9. John S. Murray et al., Process of Dispute Resolution: The Role of Lawyers 592 (1989).
10. *Id.* at 613.

This process is both structured and flexible. The structure comes from the history of the process itself, as well as from the procedural agreement that the parties sign when they enter into the mini-trial process. The flexibility comes from the parties' ability to design the process to meet their particular needs. It is private and, if successful, results in a contractually binding agreement.

> The concept underlying the minitrial is that it provides each business executive with a crash course in the merits of the dispute — a brief, but firsthand view of the best case that can be put forward by the attorneys for both sides, supplemented, if necessary, by the views of a neutral. Armed with this information, as well as their knowledge of the business relationships of the parties, the executives are equipped to negotiate a resolution of their dispute that makes business sense.[11]

"The minitrial captured the imagination of corporate executives, at least in part because it put them rather than their lawyers in control of the outcome. . . . It turns legal disputes into business decisions."[12] In business disputes the process can take a variety of forms:

> [T]he companies involved may decide to use a neutral person simply as a referee, or they may ask for an opinion about how the case would fare in court. Or the parties may ask the person to become actively involved in mediating a resolution. Finally, the principals may decide to dispense with an outsider completely and preside over the minitrial themselves."[13]

Many lawyers like the mini-trial process because they still have the opportunity to use their repertoire of persuasive advocacy skills, which can be inhibited in mediation.

Some have called this process an "information exchange," rather than a mini-trial, because the former seems more descriptive. And it has its limitations. "A minitrial is not suitable for every case, particularly those with high emotional stakes and those that involve a legal issue for which the parties want an interpretation of a statute or a binding precedent. These cases may best be resolved in court."[14]

---

11. Goldberg et al., *supra* note 2, at 230.

12. Linda R. Singer, Settling Disputes: Conflict Resolution in Business, Families, and The Legal System 61 (2d ed. 1994).

13. *Id.* at 64.

14. Lavinia Hall, ed., Negotiation Strategies for Mutual Gain: The Basic Seminar of the Program on Negotiation at Harvard Law School 56 (1993).

121

Summary Jury Trial

"The summary jury trial is an adaptation of the minitrial for cases in which the parties want more direct information about likely jury reaction than they would receive from the prediction of a minitrial neutral advisor."[15] This process is another form of abbreviated trial, with the addition of a jury. Counsel for each party makes a summary presentation of admissible evidence and arguments before a judge or other neutral and a six- or twelve-member jury. The jurors are drawn from the regular jury pool. They render an advisory (nonbinding) verdict.

Someone with decisionmaking authority from each party must be present to observe the presentation of evidence and the determination of the jury. This provides them with a realistic view of their position as they prepare for final settlement negotiations. The attorneys are permitted to question the jurors regarding why and how they reached their decision. This inquiry aids the attorneys in further trial preparation but, more importantly, helps the parties see how a future jury might view their case.

The summary jury trial can be public or private, voluntary or involuntary (judge-ordered), and is nonbinding. Since it is still relatively costly and time-consuming, it is more likely to be used in large, complex cases that would require extended trial time.

If the matter is not settled as a result of the summary jury trial and ultimately has to go to trial, a different jury hears the case, although the same judge may or may not preside over the trial. The originator of this process, Judge Thomas Lambros of the U.S. District Court for the Northern District of Ohio, believes that the procedure should remain sufficiently flexible "to accommodate the needs and styles of its various users."[16]

In a number of federal court districts, the summary jury trial is a prominent part of court-annexed dispute resolution.[17] But in others, questions remain.

> In fact, there has been extensive litigation in the federal courts over whether federal district court judges have authority, either under the Federal Rules of Civil Procedure or under the courts' inherent powers, to compel attendance of the parties, as opposed to their attorneys, at the SJT [See, e.g., *In re NLO. Inc.*, 5 F.3d 154 (6th Cir. 1993); *Strandell v. Jackson Co.*, 838 F.2d 884 (7th Cir. 1987) (district judges cannot require partici-

---

15. Goldberg et al., *supra* note 2, at 235.

16. Thomas Lambros, Summary Jury Trial — an Alternative Method of Resolving Disputes, 69 Judicature 286, 286-290 (1986).

17. Paul L. Tractenberg, New Jersey Dispute Resolution: A Lawyer's Guide to State and Federal Court Programs 441 (1994).

pation in SJT); compare *Official Airlines Guides, Inc. v. Goss,* 6 F.3d 1485 (9th Cir. 1993); *G. Heileman Brewing Co. v. Joseph Oat Corp.,* 871 F.2d 648 (7th Cir. 1989) (district judges can order settlement-empowered litigants, who are represented by counsel, to attend pretrial settlement conference)].[18]

Generally, however, the use of summary jury trials as a settlement technique is expanding across jurisdictional lines.

Judge Enslen of the U.S. district court in Michigan used summary jury trials in two interesting cases. One was a complex waste dumping case with 93 claims. The plaintiff and the defendant each picked their best case and the judge picked one case in between. The three cases went to three different summary juries. Once these three *boundary* cases were settled, the outcomes and information were used to settle all the other 90 cases.

Another interesting summary jury case involved a baby who was severely burned by very hot water. The plaintiff sued the manufacturer of the heater, claiming that the temperature valve was defective. The case was sent to a summary jury trial and the jury found for the defendant. When the parties spoke with the jury afterward, the jury told them that although the baby was terribly injured they did not think that the defendant was responsible. The jury, however, made it clear that if they had found liability, they would have awarded huge damages. The defendant's lawyer then told his client that although this jury did not find him liable one could not predict what another jury might do if the case were to be taken to court. He advised his client that it was his moral responsibility to give some money to the plaintiff; some would call this public relations. The defendant paid several hundred thousand dollars, the case was settled and did not go to court. This is another example of an imaginative resolution where both the defendant and the plaintiff were able to get most of what they wanted.[19]

Judge Lambros indicates that

[t]he decision to use summary jury trial rarely turns on the substantive legal aspects of a case, but rather depends upon the dynamics of the controversy. . . . The psychological effect of "courtroom combat" is important with regard to litigants who are either too stubborn to see their opponent's point of view, or who feel that settlement would be an admission of weakness and would prefer to have their "day in court." Any trial, however long or short, exacts some sacrifice or penalty from the litigants in the form of financial costs and emotional stress. Some litigants have the ability to handle that stress, others do not. The summary jury trial pro-

18. *Id.* at 441.
19. Sander, *supra* note 14, at 56-57.

vides a forum in which the litigant can get a taste of the trial ahead and thereby more logically evaluate his or her position.[20]

In either the mini-trial or the summary jury trial, the paralegal might be asked to prepare the agreement to participate in the process or the agreement reached as a result of its successful conclusion. In either situation, precision and accuracy and the ability to reflect the desires of the clients is paramount. Further, one must be certain that all possible contingencies are addressed. A poorly drafted agreement can lead to further disagreement.

Focus Groups

A focus group is not so much an alternative dispute resolution process as it is another settlement technique. However, since law firms are using focus groups, it behooves the paralegal to be familiar with the concept. Like other settlement tools, a focus group can take many forms, but it is similar to a summary jury trial. The major difference is that it is done outside the courtroom and only one side of the litigation is present.

For example, party *A* sues party *B*. Trial is approaching and counsel for party *A* wants to get a better grasp on how a jury might view his case. This can be accomplished by presenting a shortened version of the trial to a jury that is paid to sit and listen to the trial and reach a verdict like any other jury. However, instead of party *B* and their lawyers participating, someone from party *A*'s firm role-plays party *B*'s part. The jury hears both sides of the case, reaches a verdict, and can then be questioned by counsel as to why they reached that verdict. The jury can also be divided before deliberations and return two separate verdicts, sometimes diametrically opposed.

A focus group is considered a settlement tool because, as it gives the law firm and the client a more realistic view of their case and their chances in court, it can frequently lead to a reasonable early settlement.

Neutral Expert Factfinding

This process of dispute resolution uses a neutral third party to make recommendations based upon her expertise. The *expertise* of the neutral is the most important aspect here. The process can take on a variety of forms. It can be voluntary (generally private and outside the judicial sys-

---

20. Murray, *supra* note 9, at 652.

tem) or involuntary (court-ordered), and is nonbinding. The expert, however, may submit the findings to the judge.

The precise form the process takes seems to depend on its origination. "Early neutral evaluation" is court-ordered and

> calls for an assessment of the case early in its history by an experienced neutral on the basis of brief presentations by both sides. If the case does not settle, the assessment is kept confidential, and the evaluator helps the parties to simplify and tailor the case for more expeditious handling in trial. Sometimes the evaluator also assists the parties in monitoring discovery requests.[21]

> When business disagreements result from differing views of critical scientific, technical, business, or even legal information, the parties may be able to negotiate their own settlement, with or without a mediator, if they can resolve their conflicting perceptions. What they often need is an outside expert, whose knowledge and impartiality they all respect, to give an unbiased opinion.[22]

Furthermore, "[i]n complicated disagreements over faulty construction, medical malpractice, personal injuries, patent and securities regulation, and antitrust violations, neutral experts can help disputants to understand what is at issue and to make informed decisions concerning their liability."[23]

Sometimes "the expert may mediate, though more often [he] simply provides the parties with an impartial opinion of the facts or applicable standards or a prediction of which party would be found at fault in a trial or administrative proceeding."[24] The proceeding is more investigatory and informal rather than tied to the rules of evidence. Finally, the procedure, as used in this context, is generally private.

A rather different form of the process is found in public-sector employment disputes.

> Under some statutes, "interest" disputes not settled by mediation are submitted to a "fact-finder," who after hearing evidence from the parties makes a recommendation for the resolution of all the issues in dispute. See, e.g., 43 Pa. Stat. §1101.801. 1101.802; 150E Mass. Gen. Laws §9. . . . A unique feature of the fact-finding process is that the recommendations of the fact-finder are usually made public. The goal is for the resulting public scrutiny and pressure of "public opinion" to make it more difficult for the parties to reject the fact-finder's recommendations. See, e.g., Or.

---

21. Goldberg et al., *supra* note 2, at 251.
22. Singer, *supra* note 12, at 65.
23. *Id.* at 69.
24. *Id.* at 25.

Rev. Stat. §243.722(3), (4) (fact-finder's recommendations shall be "publicized" unless parties agree to accept them or agree to submit the dispute to final and binding arbitration).[25]

Factfinding may be just one stage of the dispute resolution process in this field. It may be followed by mediation, arbitration, or litigation.

The paralegal can assist by researching qualifications of neutrals to determine the appropriateness of their expertise. He might also develop and maintain a database of expert neutrals for future use by the law firm. In preparation of the attorney's presentation to the neutral expert, the paralegal's organizing and research skills are important resources. Once a settlement is reached, the paralegal can assist in preparing the settlement agreement.

Early Settlement/Bar Paneling

In this process, which takes place within the court structure, attorneys, with or without their clients present, meet with a panel of volunteer attorneys who hear a summary of the case and make suggestions regarding settlement. If the clients are not present at the discussions, the attorneys take the panel's suggestions back to them. The expertise and authority of the panel depends on their being familiar with practice in the pertinent subject matter as well as geographic area. The panel can therefore be relied on to predict, with some degree of accuracy, the outcome of a judicial hearing. Bar paneling frequently occurs in subject matter specialties, such as matrimonial law or medical malpractice.

In Essex County, New Jersey, it is reported that bar paneling in the matrimonial court, which started in the late 1970s, has relieved backlog and grown to employ a full-time program coordinator, and has expanded from one panel a month to two or three panels a week, scheduling between 60 and 80 cases a month. Attorneys serve voluntarily as panelists and they report a success rate of over 60 percent.[26]

25. Murray et al., *supra* note 9, at 606-607.
26. James E. Lubarsky, A Program That Works, Chronicle (Essex County Bar Foundation) Jan.-Feb., 1994.

Noncourt-Related Nonadjudicative Processes

Ombudsperson

The use of an ombudsperson is a private, voluntary, and investigatory process in which an individual is appointed to hear disputes or complaints and sometimes to make recommendations as to how to resolve them. The services of an ombudsperson are used by corporations, educational institutions, hospitals, and similar entities having a large or complicated organization. An ombudsperson, who is usually an employee of the corporation or institution, hears complaints of employees of the corporation or others who are within the institution. Making this service available represents an attempt by the organization to provide a system to deal with employee, patient, or customer complaints. Initially, the ombudsperson may serve as a mediator. If that is not successful, the ombudsperson may make a recommendation as to how the dispute should be resolved, which is generally nonbinding. The process is of an informal nature.

One expert has defined an ombudsperson as

a neutral or impartial manager within a corporation, who may provide confidential and informal assistance to managers and employees in resolving work-related concerns, who may serve as a counselor, go-between, mediator, fact-finder or upward-feedback mechanism, and whose office is located outside ordinary line management structures. . . . In technical terminology, the ombudsman is committed to integrative solutions, and avoids distributive solutions both by the design of the office (an informal, nonadjudicatory structure) and by personal commitment. . . . Most ombuds practitioners report to the CEO or someone close to the CEO.[27]

Another expert has observed:

Most U.S. ombudspeople work for the organizations they monitor. Yet they remain outside of the ordinary chains of command and generally report to the chief executive officer of a company or agency. . . . In explaining how they can be neutral when they work for the employer who is part of a dispute, these people say that their job is to assure employees of fair process and that their loyalty to the employer is satisfied when they

27. Mary P. Rowe, The Corporate Ombudsman: An Overview and Analysis, *in* Negotiation Theory and Practice 433-434 (J. William Breslin & Jeffrey Z. Rubin eds., 1993).

settle disputes among employees evenhandedly. . . . Some ombudspeople believe that their additional role of undertaking independent investigations and recommending changes to management, gives them more visibility and clout than in-house mediators have and helps to compensate for the possible effect on their credibility of the fact that they are insiders.[28]

One ombudsperson[29] lists the principal functions of an ombudsman as follows:

1. Dealing with feelings
2. Giving and receiving information on a one-to-one basis[30]
3. Counseling and problem-solving to help the manager or employee help himself or herself
4. Shuttle diplomacy
5. Mediation
6. Investigation
7. Adjudication or arbitration (rare)
8. Upward feedback[31]

In discussing what types of problems come to an ombudsperson to handle, she includes the following:

> salary and benefits; promotion and demotion; performance appraisals; job security and retirement issues; company policies; discipline/termination; discrimination and harassment; safety, ethics and whistleblowing; transfers; personality conflicts/meanness; information/referral; suggestions; working conditions; personal health, mentoring, and counseling issues; management practices; bizarre behavior and problems.[32]

Ombudspeople hail from a variety of backgrounds, including human resources, legal, technical, and managerial roles. As in many dispute resolution processes, the role played by the ombudsperson varies with each setting. However, its flexibility and value make it a viable profession in dispute resolution.

---

28. Singer, *supra* note 12, at 25-26, 100, 101-102.

29. Rowe, *supra* note 27, at 436-438.

30. "[A]n ombudsman is likely to be the bellwether or early warning device for whatever problems the employer has not yet met, but will soon have to deal with. Examples of such problems include sexual harassment in the early 1970s, AIDS in the early 1980s, and now new kinds of drug problems." *Id.* at 436.

31. "Possibly the most important function of the ombudsman is to receive, perhaps analyze, then pass along information that will foster timely change in a company." *Id.* at 438.

32. *Id.* at 441.

In North America, there are about 100 ombuds offices in colleges and universities, an estimated 200 in corporations. Three dozen newspapers have an ombudsman. Nearly 4,000 hospitals have patient ombuds offices and a great many businesses have client or consumer complaint offices. Each state has a nursing home/long-term care ombuds structure, and there appear to be about 1,500 part-time and full-time ombudspeople attached to those offices. In addition, there are perhaps two dozen classical ombuds offices in states, provinces and cities, and scattered practitioners for prisons and other institutions. Some radio and television stations and newspapers also have citizen's complaint or citizen's service structures, as do also mayors' and governors' offices.[33]

A paralegal within a corporation or institution could be called upon to help develop an ombuds structure for the corporate employer, become an ombudsperson, or to work in the ombuds office.

Conciliation

The *American Heritage Dictionary* defines "conciliate" as "to overcome the distrust or animosity of; win over; placate; soothe or to gain, win, or secure by friendly overtures; from the Latin *conciliare,* to bring together, unite. . . ." Conciliation occurs when a third-party neutral gathers disputants at a meeting to discuss their conflicts.

While some consider conciliation to be synonymous with mediation, it is not. Conciliation is usually limited to getting the parties to communicate, either face-to-face or through other measures. The conciliator does not necessarily participate in that communication. "Unlike mediation, conciliation, or convening, usually connotes only preliminary involvement by a third party. The outsider may bring the parties together or carry a few messages back and forth."[34] Mediation, on the other hand, is usually face-to-face, and the mediator facilitates the active communication of the parties in an attempt to resolve their differences.

Conciliation as a form of dispute resolution is most often found in an international context.

33. *Id.* at 445.
34. Singer, *supra* note 12, at 24.

Facilitation

Facilitation is a process that involves a group of people trying to resolve differences or strategize or plan for future endeavors. The facilitator uses a variety of techniques to enhance, organize, and direct communication so that the group may move forward, either out of the conflict or toward a particular goal. "Facilitators may act as moderators in large meetings, making sure that everyone is able to speak and be heard. Facilitators are not expected to volunteer their own ideas or participate actively in moving parties toward agreement."[35] Facilitators may do extensive preliminary work in meeting with various subgroups to develop an agenda and focus the subgroups. Generally, the facilitator does not have a stake in the outcome of the group endeavor, but rather has an interest in the success of the process itself.

Summary

There are a number of variations on the themes of negotiation, mediation, and arbitration. Some are used only in particular settings and others are used sparingly, but in a broader range of applications.

The adjudicative processes are private judging, med-arb, and final-offer arbitration. These are all private and the parties pay the neutral's fees. All are subject to process criticism, as well as to the parties' affirmation. *Private judging* arises through the consent of the parties or direction of the court. The latter occurs in complex matters with trial pending. In some states, decisions are filed with the court and are subject to appeal; in others they are not, depending upon statute. *Med-arb* is a creature of contract. It is a combination of mediation first, followed by arbitration if the parties cannot agree in mediation. The same neutral serves in both roles. An award is private and is treated the same as other arbitration awards. *Final-offer arbitration* is used largely in public employee interest and baseball player salary disputes. Each party submits a final offer and the neutral must select one of the offers. The results may be made public because of citizen interest.

There are also nonadjudicative processes. These can be further subdivided into those relating to litigation and those that are not litigation inspired. They can be private or court annexed. The first five —

35. *Ibid.*

minitrial, summary jury trial, focus groups, neutral expert factfinding, and early settlement/bar paneling — are considered "settlement techniques" intended to get the parties to objectively view their case and consider the benefits of settlement.

Both the *mini-trial* and *summary jury trial* are abbreviated versions of a trial, presented by counsel before a neutral and before the parties or their representatives who have decisionmaking authority. Summary jury trial is before a jury, whose members can be questioned about the verdict. After the trial, the parties negotiate toward settlement with the added advantage of having seen a summary of their case tried. The use of *focus groups* to serve as jurors is similar to the summary jury trial, except (1) only one side of the litigation is responsible for the mock trial, (2) it is done privately outside the court system, and (3) the jurors are paid.

When a neutral is brought in as an *expert,* his role is to hear the case and help the parties agree on technical disputes that may require the input of an expert. The expert also makes nonbinding recommendations. *Bar paneling* uses the good offices of volunteer attorneys who hear abbreviated presentations of the case from counsel and then help settlement negotiations through suggestions based on their expertise and knowledge of the court.

Noncourt-related, nonadjudicative processes include the role of *ombudsperson, conciliator,* and *facilitator.* The former is usually an employee of a corporation or institution who hears conflicts within the organization or conflicts between the organization and others, i.e., customers. In this role, the ombudsperson serves as an investigator, mediator, teacher, and diplomat, attempting to resolve conflict and keep the employer informed about problems, without involving the employer in the particular problem. A conciliator, on the other hand, is a neutral who brings the disputing parties together to discuss their differences, but may not necessarily participate in those discussions. A *facilitator* works with groups to guide and enhance their discussions to work through a dispute or plan for a future endeavor.

EXERCISES

1. Research your state court to determine which of the processes described in this chapter are being used within the court system, either court annexed or court referred.

2. Do the same research as above for the federal district in which you reside.

3. Do the same research as above, but with reference to private dispute resolution applications available.

4. Develop a chart based on the foregoing research that indicates what processes are being used, where they are being used, and, finally, for what types of disputes (labor, contract, family, medical malpractice, etc.).

5. Observe and report on one of the processes being used to resolve an actual conflict.

6. Develop several hypothetical conflicts in which you would use one of the processes described in this chapter. In a class discussion, ask other students which process they would apply. Discuss which process is most appropriate and why.

7. Do research using one of the dispute resolution journals regarding an ethical or policy issue in one of the processes discussed in this chapter.

8. Interview a neutral who has participated in these processes and ask him or her to compare several of the ADR processes.

9. Develop a role play for students in the class to act out and apply one of the processes.

Policy, Ethical, and Practice Issues

Self-Determination
Maintaining the Integrity of the Process
Fees, Advertising, and Solicitation
A Practice Issue: Who Attends Mediation?
Summary
Exercises

Introduction

As in any field of endeavor, issues of policy, ethics, education, and application are debated among the practitioners, policymakers, and academics. These debates contribute to the molding of the future of the field. They also reflect the vitality and growth of the profession.

This chapter presents current thinking on *some* of these issues and encourages the student to research others and to keep abreast of emerging questions and debates in the discipline. Thoughtful, critical consideration of policy and professional issues contributes to the development of each student's ethical self.

In reviewing these materials, one will find that there is some necessary overlap among the policy, ethical, and practice issues. How they are distinguished will depend on the perspective adopted. Some issues are policy considerations, to be made by program developers in conjunction with providers and clients; others are ethical issues for individual mediators (but are affected by policy decisions); and one is a practice issue (but could be included in policy decisions).

Policy Issues

Institutionalizing ADR Systems Within the Court System

There is thoughtful concern in some dispute resolution circles regarding the current trend towards integrating ADR systems into the court structure and mandating its use. Court-connected ADR abounds, including mandatory custody mediation, landlord-tenant mediation, mandatory automobile arbitration, and settlement weeks, among others. There are also court-referred programs, where the rules provide for referral by the court system to an outside nonprofit or for-profit provider. At the other end of the spectrum, noncourt-connected ADR includes private community mediation centers, for-profit individual providers, peer mediation in educational settings, as well as corporate providers.

Proponents of ADR integration within the court system say that it benefits both the courts and the disputants and demonstrates the legal system's support of these alternative methods. Proponents further argue that by having the systems in place within the court structure, both attorneys and disputants will be more familiar with them. Those ADR systems that are within the court structure are usually funded by court fees. Judges and lawyers are more likely to support the use of systems that are part of the court structure and over which they have better control.

Those opposed to such ADR integration say that the mere structuring of ADR systems, particularly mediation, will cause ADR to lose the flexibility and spontaneity that makes it a valuable alternative. That is to say, by integrating ADR systems into the courts, those systems will become as rigidly structured as the courts. Further, integration will place ADR under the control of lawyers and judges, which will alter the nature of ADR. It will have an effect on private providers of ADR services, whose services and activities would otherwise be controlled by their own professional ethical standards and the market.

While defenders of ADR integration argue that it will not necessarily limit the development of private ADR providers, it would appear that a certain formalism occurs once the bar firmly has control over the systems. For example, in Chicago, the bar has a separate corporation that trains providers and manages all ADR in the court system, except in the family area. (Family mediation in many areas is provided by mental health care professionals.) The only private ADR that is taking place in Chicago is in the upper levels of complex costly commercial disputes.

Some opposed to private ADR are concerned that ADR firms that solicit retired judges to serve as neutrals are pulling those judges away from public service in the judiciary and depleting valuable personnel resources. There appears, however, to be little support for this position.

Mandatory vs. Voluntary Participation in ADR Within the Court System

This is a subissue of the foregoing. As courts and bar associations, with all good intent, seem bent on ADR integration, we see the man-

135

dating of use of those ADR systems that are in place. A point of clarification here: "Mandates to participate in a dispute resolution process should be distinguished from coercion to settle once participation has begun."[1] "Mandatory" is applied to those processes in which "the third-party neutral lacks authority to issue a binding decision, such as mediation, conciliation, early neutral evaluation, moderated settlement conferences, and summary jury trials, and with processes in which parties can reject the award and assert the right to trial, such as court-annexed arbitration."[2]

In an attempt to face the issues that mandatory ADR raises, the Law and Public Policy Committee of the Society of Professionals in Dispute Resolution developed seven recommendations. (See Appendix D, page 177.) To summarize, it was recommended first that the developers of court systems take into consideration not just the efficient running of the judicial system, but the needs of the parties and the public interest. Specifically, any established system should not harm historically disenfranchised groups. It should not be just another step to go through before one gets to court. It must not be a wholesale transferal where all cases, or all cases of one type, are sent to mandatory ADR. Optimally, cases should be sent to specific ADR programs on a case-by-case basis.

Recommendation number two states that "[f]unding for mandatory dispute resolution programs should be provided on a basis comparable to funding for trials." This is to avoid an unfair burden on people who use ADR.

Recommendation three addresses financial disincentives to trial when a disputant chooses not to settle in mediation or to seek a trial de novo after arbitration. Such disincentives should not be used in mediation and should be clearly described in mandatory arbitration.

Number four provides: "Mandatory participation should be used only when a high quality program (i) is readily accessible, (ii) permits party participation, (iii) permits lawyer participation when the parties wish it, and (iv) provides clarity about the precise procedures that are being required." This is self-explanatory. Two additional points are in the Comments section of the Report: (1) When possible, the culture, race, and gender diversity in the selection of neutrals is an appropriate objective; and (2) if the process is provided outside of the court system, the court should maintain oversight.

Recommendation five dictates that all who will regularly be af-

1. Mandated Participation and Settlement Coercion: Dispute Resolution as it Relates to the Courts, Report #1 of the Law and Public Policy Committee of the Society of Professionals in Dispute Resolution, Washington, D.C. (1991), at 6.
2. *Ibid.*

fected by mandatory dispute resolution should participate in the planning. This includes attorneys, judges, court personnel, dispute resolution providers, and the *public*. After establishment, programs should be monitored and if they are not meeting the needs of participants, they should be discontinued.

Recommendation six states: "Procedures for compulsory referrals should include, to the extent feasible, case assessment by a person knowledgeable about dispute resolution procedures and should provide for timely consideration of motions for exclusion." The latter is particularly important. Such motions should be taken seriously and heard in a timely manner to avoid possible harm or wasting of time.

Recommendation seven recognizes that failure to attend or participate in even mandatory procedures can sometimes be a problem and proposes that sanctions need to be imposed. However, the behavior for which sanctions are imposed must be clearly defined, not failure to "bargain in good faith" or participation in a "meaningful manner."

Unless the institutionalization of mandatory ADR becomes a deeply embedded reality, this controversy will continue to be discussed. However, once a system has been institutionalized for ten years or more, people tend to accept it as a reality and not to question it. This ten-year anniversary for ADR is approaching in some jurisdictions. Therefore, continued study and review is essential.

The "Dark Side" of ADR

ADR has its critics. They believe that processes that keep disputes and their resolution private harm the public. In certain situations, that is true. An example would be if a company harms an individual with a new product but resolves the resulting personal injury lawsuit privately, the product could conceivably continue to harm other consumers. Likewise, charges of pollution that are mediated without all the necessary parties present can result in harm to those not present. However, in considering this argument, we must keep in mind that even when parties litigate, they can settle their litigation and keep the terms of the settlement private.

Another criticism is that because of private settlement, some of the legal reform and development that comes about through judicial decisions is lost. Suppose, for example, that the legal issues surrounding a person's right to die or a surrogate parent's right to keep her child were not decided in the courts and not brought to public attention. The public would have no guideposts for behavior in those situations in the absence of judicial decision or legislative fiat.

Similarly, there is concern about those disputants who are sufficiently weak in comparison to the other party that, without protection, they will suffer. The stronger party is able to intimidate, harass, and generally impose their will on the less powerful. If representatives (such as attorneys or other advocates) are not present to protect the powerless, and the neutral is unable or unwilling, due to other constraints, to protect them,[3] has the legal community put such weaker parties in jeopardy by permitting ADR to deal with their conflict? One response to this criticism is that the court is not always effective in dealing with such power imbalances. For example, a powerful corporation has the financial ability to hire the brightest and best legal counsel and has the time to delay litigation in defense against a poor consumer who cannot afford an hourly legal bill sufficient to properly deal with the corporate defendant. Nor can the consumer wait out the delaying tactics.

Let us look at one more criticism of ADR, particularly court-mandated ADR. In many instances, it imposes another step in the legal process. This results in additional delays, lost time from work, and frustration for the parties. Entire classes of cases — for example, all damage cases under a certain dollar amount — are sent to arbitration. The parties appear, present their case, and the arbitrator makes an award. If the parties are dissatisfied with the award, they must so notify the court and come back for a trial de novo. This is frequently done in the "less significant" cases, thereby creating a "second class" justice system. Even those who strongly support ADR and its use cannot deny this problem exists and requires attention.

This discussion does not exhaust the criticisms that have been leveled at ADR. Rather it is meant to raise issues, alert the student, and aid in the student's critical analysis of the field.

To Regulate or Not to Regulate?

State regulation of ADR providers, particularly private mediators, is a topic of current interest. Those in favor of regulation cite the need to protect uninformed consumers from unscrupulous or untrained mediators, the absence of professional self-regulation, and the lack of consistency in the background and training of existing private providers. Providers of court-annexed mediation generally have to meet certain minimum standards in training and/or experience and/or education

---

3. The neutral may be unwilling to intervene because of the commitment to impartiality. See *infra* at page 146.

background. The standards are higher for providers of family/custody mediation within the court system.

Certain professional groups, such as the Society of Professionals in Dispute Resolution and the Academy of Family Mediators, for example, publish professional standards. And although no state licenses private ADR providers at this time, some states do have a mediator certification system in place. The problem with setting standards, however, is that it is difficult to clearly measure the diverse attributes of competent ADR providers, which include maturity, sensitivity, education, subject matter expertise, and well-developed communication skills.

Since the profession is still relatively young, it may be too early for states to license or regulate ADR providers' credentials or mandate certain education or training of private ADR professionals. However, it is incumbent upon the profession to maintain high standards of service and education to avoid public criticism. Further, the profession has a responsibility to educate the public regarding provider training and standards of professional conduct. This is an area that requires continued research, development, and scrutiny.

How Is Success Measured?

Court-annexed ADR has been touted as relieving court congestion, saving money, and providing a more informal process for the disputant. Has it done this and should it do this? In developing a program, the initiators must first determine what they are trying to accomplish and why. For example, are they looking to increase the public's satisfaction with the legal process or are they looking to reduce the court's expenditures and ease court congestion? Are they looking to avoid the need to appoint more judges? Their reasons may be all of these and more. However, they need to be clear on their goals. Only then can a system be properly developed to meet their goals and studied to determine if the goals have been met.

If the system of ADR that is developed meets the goals, then it is successful. If it does not, then one must determine whether it satisfies other goals or should be eliminated in whole or in part. It is not sufficient to say ADR is a good thing and everyone else is doing it and, therefore, we want to do it too.

This issue is raised in another context, particularly in mediation. If the court, or the funding source in community mediation, determines success by number of cases that reach settlement within the shortest period of time, a great disservice has been done to all involved. Effective mediation takes time — to hear the parties, to permit them to vent anger and frustration if necessary, to enable them to develop their own resolution, and to learn to work with each other. A mediator who is being judged by the number of cases settled will most likely be more intrusive and controlling in the mediation and less likely to adequately listen to the parties and their needs.

Further, settlement can occur after the mediation process is abandoned because the parties were at least given the opportunity to hear each other. Thus, even when matters are not resolved, parties have expressed satisfaction with the process. Perhaps some parties feel listened to and empowered. Perhaps some disputants learn to communicate better as a result of the mediation. The value of mediation is very difficult to measure and imposing unreasonable time constraints limits its viability as an effective process.

Considering the length of time a case may take to mediate, particularly a community matter where the parties have an ongoing relationship, some critics of ADR point to the fact that it would take less time in court. However, they are not looking at the larger picture. Is the court better able to deal with the disputants in such a way as to dissuade their return to court on another matter. Does the court deal with the underlying interpersonal conflict that can erupt later with another "cause"? In mediation, the parties may come to a better understanding of each other, may learn to communicate better with each other, or may decide that they do not like each other and have no wish to continue a relationship. Whatever the result, the parties have decided the outcome, not the court; this alone empowers the parties.

Policy/Ethical Issues

Some concerns in the field of dispute resolution have both a policy impact on the planners and developers of an ADR program, as well as an ethical impact on the individual practitioners. We have already considered the example of how a mediator must face time constraints or be expected to reach a "success quota of settlements" while at the same time trying to adequately mediate a lengthy, involved, and heated conflict that will take substantially more time than he can afford to give. Without the beneficial settlement statistics, the ADR program might lose funding; but without time spent on this particular case, it will not be resolved, or the resolution will not "stick" because all the issues have not been dealt with. Therefore, it is incumbent upon developers of programs to not let settlement statistics "run the program."

This section considers similar policy/ethical issues.

Is ADR Appropriate in All Types of Cases?

This is another issue in which there are strongly held beliefs on both sides. Here we consider but two examples of the debate.

DOMESTIC VIOLENCE

Many people who work in the area of domestic violence strongly oppose the use of mediation; some even go so far as to advocate that it be categorically rejected. First, however, in any particular case, one must look more critically at the issues involved.

Is there a history of domestic violence between the couple, or one incident? A history of violence puts the dispute and its resolution in a different category. It is likely that there is a severe power imbalance and that the victim is terrified of the abuser and has a very diminished capacity to negotiate on her own behalf. Where this is true, mediation probably is inappropriate. If there has been only a single, relatively minor incident of domestic violence, and the parties appear to be able to confront each other and deal with each other, then mediation may be appropriate and beneficial.

Determining the frequency of domestic violence, or its effects on the parties, can prove to be very difficult for the mediator or for those who are screening the cases. And some legal professionals will raise a further question: Is there merely an allegation of domestic violence to gain an advantage in litigation, or is it real? This is also difficult to determine and may be beyond the mediator's abilities.

Related to the issue of the existence of domestic violence or its frequency is the general question of whether or not these cases *can be* screened out of mediation. Most people are ashamed of domestic violence in their families and will not openly admit its occurrence. Therefore, the mediator may not even be aware of domestic violence or may first become aware of it during the mediation.

What is being mediated — parenting arrangements, financial issues, or the continuance of the relationship (and, therefore, the violence itself)? Most people maintain that the violence itself cannot be mediated. The answer to whether other issues can be mediated when domestic violence has occurred may go back to the question of whether there is too great a power imbalance between the parties.

> Mediation . . . places the parties on equal footing and asks them to negotiate an agreement for future behavior. Beyond failing to punish assailants for their crimes, this process implies that victims share responsibility for the illegal conduct and requires them to modify their own behavior in exchange for the assailants' promises not to commit further crimes.[4]

Mediation of the violent acts is clearly a subversion of the law and a violation of the victim, which cannot be tolerated.

Does this mean that mediation simply cannot work in cases of domestic violence? Some say yes. But those who support continued attempts at mediation where domestic violence has occurred say no. The latter individuals point to ongoing violence in our society and throughout the world and hold up mediation as one possible solution that must continue to be available and that has the potential to transform the parties.

By removing all domestic violence cases from mediation, is the ADR community giving up on self-determination and transformation through mediation? This is less a practice issue and more a philosophical one. One of the reasons mediation is so powerful is that it gives the dispute and its resolution back to the parties. It empowers them to reach their own resolution of the conflict. It demonstrates to them the skills necessary to deal with future conflicts. However, parties must be ready and open to such benefits, and victims and perpetrators of domestic violence are not likely to possess that openness. One proposal is to not mandate mediation in cases of domestic violence, but to permit the parties — with knowledge of the process, advice of counsel, and support of therapy — to request mediation. This, of course, excludes those who do not have the necessary financial or experiential resources.

SEXUAL HARASSMENT GRIEVANCES

Related in concept to the issue of domestic violence, but not in application, is the question of whether sexual harassment grievances in the workplace should be submitted to mediation prior to going to arbitration. Once again, one must approach with caution. One professional maintains that

---

4. Lisa G. Lerman, Mediation of Wife Abuse Cases: The Adverse Impact of Informal Dispute Resolution on Women, 7 Harv. Women's L.J. 57, 72 (1984), *quoting* United States Commission on Civil Rights, under the Rule of Thumb: Battered Women and the Administration of Justice 1 (1982).

sexual harassment cases are similar in power structure to domestic violence or criminal assault matters. In those cases there is more than a simple dispute over money or property. Instead, there is a dynamic present that involves power, fear, and coercion. These elements underlie the "dispute" being mediated. . . . But like an iceberg, only the tip is visible, and the most dangerous part remains unseen. In those situations, there is an imbalance of power between the batterer and the victim that cannot be reconciled in mediation. Many legal commentators have concluded that mediation is inappropriate in these cases unless special circumstances are present. Because the same dynamic exists between harasser and victim, mediation is also inappropriate in sexual harassment grievance cases.[5]

Similar to the question of whether mediation "covers up" the crime of spousal abuse when it is used to resolve cases of domestic violence, there is concern that the actions of a harasser in the workplace will go unpunished in mediation. "Grievance mediation of these cases, no matter how well intended, risks trivializing the seriousness of sexual harassment and maintaining an inhospitable environment for the female workforce."[6]

Of equal importance is the process of clearly defining the behavior that constitutes sexual harassment. Lack of definition creates uncertainty about what kind of behavior is acceptable. Such a definition cannot continue to be refined through case law if the behavior is mediated and therefore does not come before the court or the public. Sexual harassment cases that are "settled" may send the wrong message to other employees, both men and women. Women may believe that future claims will not be taken seriously and men may believe that unacceptable behavior will go unpunished.

The decision to mediate sexual harassment cases cannot be made on a case-by-case basis because it is usually provided for in the employment contract. Therefore, mediation in such a case must be closely monitored as to its effectiveness.

For mediation to be accepted as an alternative to an adjudicatory process, such as grievance arbitration, the mediator must be fair, impartial, and nonjudgmental; the process must be voluntary and free of bias; and the parties must be equals in the dispute. . . . [A]dherence to this criteria is crucial for the process to be considered appropriate and legitimate.[7]

ADR policymakers need to study the appropriateness of a particular process to a particular class of cases or disputes. Not all divorce cases

---

5. Mori Irvine, Mediation: Is it Appropriate for Sexual Harassment Grievances?, 9 Ohio St. J. Dis. Resol. 28 (1993).
6. *Id.* at 28.
7. *Id.* at 32.

should be mediated — some are being arbitrated and some still need to go to trial. Perhaps one should consider a mini-trial for divorce matters. Not all business dissolutions should be arbitrated. Some should be mediated, or use a neutral expert. Not all personal injury cases should be arbitrated. Some require the gentler hand of mediation and others perhaps need the input of a summary jury trial. We need to look at the attributes of particular cases to determine the appropriateness of each process. It is important to keep open minds on this issue and not classify and categorize disputes by which ADR process is used to resolve them.

Qualification of Neutrals

A principal issue regarding the qualification of neutrals is whether the neutral needs process training. Most professionals would say there should be a requirement of at least *some* minimal training to qualify the arbitrator, mediator, or other neutral. If a neutral does not know what a mediator, for example, does and the tools he uses to do it, the neutral might end up serving as an expert factfinder instead of a mediator.

Training can be provided by the court system, an organizational provider, undergraduate or graduate school, law school, or through a variety of other training sources. Most training provides for simulations or role plays to give the student an opportunity to practice the newly learned techniques. In some programs, particularly in the law school setting, students are given the opportunity, through clinics, to serve as neutrals and to counsel clients through an ADR process. While there may be some "natural" mediators out there, just like there are some "natural" teachers, both require training.

Is it necessary for a neutral to be schooled in the theory and/or law of the process in which she serves? Probably not, but that education does provide the practitioner with a more well-developed background in the process. It acts in a way similar to experience. A mediator who has significant experience, and has thought reflectively and critically about that experience, is a more mature professional. Similarly, a mediator who has studied the mediation process from an academic perspective and participated in ethical and policy discussions in addition to having the training previously mentioned is a more well-rounded professional. Neither necessarily makes the neutral better, but perhaps richer.

Should the neutral have subject matter knowledge? Should, for example, someone who arbitrates the breakup of a professional corporation whose main asset is real estate, which must be valued, have experience in or knowledge about real estate valuation? This is a complex question which divides the experts. Some professionals maintain that an expert in the *process*, particularly mediation, has sufficient knowledge to serve. In fact, the absence of substantive knowledge is a benefit because the neutral will not be tempted to prejudge (in arbitration) or offer options (in mediation). Others say that in some complex areas — such as environmental, medical, or domestic relations — subject matter knowledge is either helpful or essential. Finally, there are those who maintain that subject matter knowledge is essential for *all* neutrals.

How one answers the question about the need for subject matter knowledge may depend on the ADR process being considered. Arbitrators, for example, may be expected to have, and frequently are chosen, for their subject matter expertise.

Ethical Issues

Ethical dilemmas are not uncommon to practitioners of ADR. The following subsections combine the SPIDR Ethical Standards of Professional Conduct[8] and those proposed by Professor Baruch Bush for use in mediation to provide some guidelines for handling those dilemmas.

General Responsibilities

The SPIDR Standards start with general responsibilities and indicate that the neutrals' duty extends to the parties, the profession, and to themselves. "They should be honest and unbiased, act in good faith, be diligent, and not seek to advance their own interest at the expense of the parties."[9]

The second part of the standards, which is directed at the neutral's more specific responsibilities to the parties, is divided into six sections: (1) impartiality, (2) informed consent, (3) confidentiality, (4) conflict of interest, (5) promptness, and (6) the settlement and its consequences.

---

8. SPIDR, Making the Tough Calls: Ethical Exercises for Neutral Dispute Resolvers (1991).
9. *Id.* at 3.

Impartiality

"Impartiality means absence of favoritism or bias — i.e., expressed sympathy or antipathy — toward any party or any position taken by a party to a mediation. In addition, it means a commitment to aid all parties, as opposed to a single party, in exploring the possibilities for resolution."[10] This applies to both verbal and nonverbal communications and actions. It often happens in an ADR setting that one party is offensive, aggressive, or intemperate while the other is quiet, less powerful, or needful of protection. The natural reaction is to try to help the party in need of protection. However, as this can interfere with the parties' self-determination and autonomy, it is essential that the neutral remain unbiased.

Clearly, where the neutral's impartiality is in question, she should decline to serve or withdraw from serving.[11]

Consent

In a mediation, a description of the process must be provided to the parties, along with their right to participate. The mediator should "avoid exerting undue pressure on a party — whether to participate in mediation or to accept a settlement; nevertheless a mediator may and should encourage parties to consider both the benefits of participation and settlement and the costs of withdrawal and impasse."[12]

This raises the issue of the parties' capacity to consent.

Where a party appears to be acting under pressure of any kind, or without fully comprehending the process, issues, or options for settlement, the mediator is obligated to explore these matters with the party and to assist them in making freely chosen and informed decisions. . . . Where a party appears to be acting under complete coercion or fear, or without capacity to comprehend the process and issues and make decisions, the mediator is obligated to explore this question and, unless the party in question objects, discontinue the mediation. If that party insists on continuing, the mediator may do so, but should continue to raise the question and check for willingness to proceed.[13]

10. Robert A. Baruch Bush, The Dilemmas of Mediation Practice: A Study of Ethical Dilemmas and Policy Implications 34 (1992).
11. *Id.* at 34.
12. *Id.* at 35.
13. *Ibid.*

The more general standards of SPIDR indicate that the "neutral has an obligation to assure that all parties understand the nature of the process, the procedures, the particular role of the neutral, and the parties' relationship to the neutral."[14] Consent is assumed in a process where either the parties have chosen it or it arises out of a contract. However, the neutral still has an obligation to explain the process and her role.

Consent can also be an issue in court-ordered arbitration, summary jury trial, or mini-trial. However, there seems to be a consensus that the courts have the authority to order participation once the parties have submitted to its jurisdiction.

Confidentiality

"Maintaining confidentiality is critical to the dispute resolution process. Confidentiality encourages candor, a full exploration of the issues and a neutral's acceptability."[15] The duty to maintain confidentiality extends to third parties not present at the mediation, such as attorneys, the courts, and referring agencies, as well as between the disputants. The mediator must keep confidential all things disclosed in caucus, unless the speaker consents to disclosure. This duty to maintain confidentiality is limited only by statutory requirements of disclosure.

The appropriate level of confidentiality that is required depends on the ADR process, its source, the preference of the parties, and any contractual provisions. For example, when arbitrating in the court system, the arbitrator provides a copy of the award and a brief summary of the matter to the court. In private arbitrations, however, the contract giving rise to the process or the rules governing the process should dictate the level of confidentiality. The neutral in these situations has the responsibility of advising the parties of the level of confidentiality that is to be maintained or, if none is set forth, of determining the desires of the parties with respect to confidentiality.

Conflict of Interest

Any neutral must avoid a conflict of interest, which is generally described as the neutral's having some business or personal connection with one of the parties or their representative. The parties must be informed and given the opportunity to seek another neutral. A more subtle prob-

---

14. SPIDR, *supra* note 8, at 3.
15. *Id.* at 3-4.

lem can arise when the neutral develops a relationship with one of the parties or their representative after the process has begun. Is the neutral prohibited from entering into such a relationship out of concern that the other party may become aware of it and believe that it predated the process and compromises the neutral's objectivity? The neutral must avoid both the appearance and the reality of a conflict.

A conflict of interest can arise in the context of the neutral's having to meet the requirement of a certain number of cases settled to satisfy a program administrator or funding source. This conflicts with the reality that not all cases settle, or settle quickly, and can adversely affect the neutral's performance. Further, a mediator who depends on the court or on attorneys for referrals may want to resolve matters in a way that she knows will be satisfactory to the referring agency. However, this may not be in the best interests of the disputants. The primary interest of the mediator must be to the disputants and to the process, not to outside third parties.

Promptness

"The neutral shall exert every reasonable effort to expedite the process."[16] This is self-explanatory.

The Settlement and Its Consequences

What should a mediator do if the parties appear to be developing an agreement that violates the law or public policy? What if the agreement appears to be grossly unfair to one of the parties?

> The dispute resolution process belongs to the parties. The neutral has no vested interest in the terms of a settlement, but must be satisfied that agreements in which he or she has participated will not impugn the integrity of the process. The neutral has a responsibility to see that the parties consider the terms of a settlement. If the neutral is concerned about the possible consequences of a proposed agreement, and the needs of the parties dictate, the neutral must inform the parties of that concern. In adhering to this standard the neutral may find it advisable to educate the parties, to refer one or more parties for specialized advice, or to withdraw from the case. In no case, however, shall the neutral violate confidentiality.[17]

16. *Id.* at 4.
17. *Ibid.*

Unrepresented Interests

Here we raise the issue of the responsibility of the neutral to consider the interests of those not present at the table. Some experts maintain that the neutral should try to obtain the participation of those who have an interest in the process but who are not present. However, if that is not possible, then the neutral should ensure that the interests of unrepresented parties have at least been considered by those present at the process.

Competence

A neutral should not accept a case in which he feels he does not possess the experience or substantive knowledge necessary to serve the disputants. Similarly, if a neutral accepts a case and thereafter determines that he does not have the sufficient knowledge to proceed, he has the responsibility to withdraw. In both situations, the neutral should inform the parties as to his limits. Finally, it is the neutral's responsibility to "obtain necessary skills and substantive training appropriate to his/her areas of practice, and to upgrade those skills on an ongoing basis."[18]

Self-Determination

This issue of self-determination relates specifically to mediation. The parties' self-determination is the cornerstone of mediation and it can be lost or impaired by a meddlesome mediator. "A mediator shall respect and encourage self-determination by the parties in their decision whether, and on what terms, to resolve their dispute, and shall refrain from being directive and judgmental regarding the issues in dispute and options for settlement.[19]

The issue of the parties' self-determination raises several significant ethical dilemmas for the practicing mediator. Professor Baruch Bush has produced the following guidelines:

A. A mediator is obligated to leave to the parties full responsibility for deciding whether, and on what terms, to resolve their dispute. S/he may

18. Baruch Bush, *supra* note 10, at 34. It should be noted here that Professor Baruch Bush's recommended standards of practice were directed toward mediators. I have taken the liberty of applying them to other neutrals as well.
19. *Id.* at 35.

and should assist them in making informed and thoughtful decisions; but s/he shall never substitute his/her judgment for that of the parties, as regards any aspect of the mediation.

B. Subject to Section A. above . . . a mediator is obligated to raise questions for the parties to consider regarding the acceptability, sufficiency, and feasibility, for all sides of proposed options for settlement — including their impact on affected third-parties. Furthermore, a mediator may make suggestions for the parties' consideration. However, at no time shall a mediator make a decision for the parties, or directly express his/her opinion about or advise for or against any proposal under consideration.

C. [I]f a party to mediation declines to consult an attorney or counselor, after the mediator has raised this option, the mediator is obligated to permit the mediation to go forward according to the parties' wishes.

D. Whenever the parties are advised by independent counsel or experts, the mediator is obligated to encourage the parties to assess such advice for themselves and make their own independent decisions.

E. If, in the mediator's judgment, an agreement reached by the parties is an agreement that a court would refuse to enforce because of illegality, substantive unconscionability, or any other reason, the mediator is obligated to so inform the parties. The mediator may choose to discontinue the mediation in such circumstance, but should not violate the obligation of confidentiality.[20]

Maintaining the Integrity of the Process

The neutral has the duty to uphold the integrity of the process. Part of that duty includes staying within the bounds of the neutral's role. For example, a mediator who is a lawyer should not give legal advice, or, if a counselor, he should not counsel the parties. Neither of these is within the role of mediator proper. A neutral can raise the option of seeking outside assistance from either type of professional, or from any others such as an accountant or a tax authority.

A further part of this responsibility to maintain the integrity of the process is to encourage other neutrals, to advocate on behalf of the process, and to educate the public. In the mediation, the mediator should encourage effective, nonjudgmental communication between the parties and should model the same. "A mediator shall encourage mutual respect between the parties, and shall take reasonable steps, subject to the principle of self-determination, to limit abuses of the mediation process."[21]

20. *Id*. at 35–36.
21. *Id*. at 36.

Fees, Advertising, and Solicitation

If fees are charged, as they are in most private ADR processes, the amount must be disclosed to the parties at the beginning of the process. It should be determined how the fee responsibility will be divided between the parties. The duty to disclose also means that advertising, where permitted, must be honest and not promise successful settlements. Furthermore, no referral fees are permitted.

A Practice Issue: Who Attends Mediation?

Numerous discussions have occurred regarding who should attend the mediation. Should the mediator permit the attorney representing the parties to participate in the mediation? Should the attorney actively participate or remain available for advice only? Should other representatives or "helpers" be permitted to observe/participate in the mediation? The answers to these questions can be a policy decision made by the sponsoring agency, one of general practice in the area, or made by the mediator across the board or on an individual basis. This author believes that if the parties want others present, and they do not inhibit or interrupt the process, they should be permitted to participate. Minimally, the decision should be made on a case-by-case basis to maintain the flexibility of the process.

Summary

Policy issues relating to ADR include whether, how much, and under what circumstances ADR should be integrated into the court system. There are arguments on both sides, involving control and resources. A major part of the argument revolves around whether litigants should be required to participate in court-annexed ADR. The issues raised are addressed in the SPIDR recommendations, which seek to retain flexibility, and open and equal access, to limit financial disincentives, to maintain high quality, to provide the parties the ability to opt out, to integrate cultural sensitivity, and to ensure the parties' participation in planning.

151

The criticisms of ADR must be evaluated and addressed. They include concern over the privacy of the process, the possibility that ADR may inhibit legal reform, the potential inability to protect weak parties, and the imposition of an additional step in the court process.

The regulation of ADR providers is another policy issue. At this time, because of the developing nature of the profession, the only regulation is for minimum training requirements for court-connected providers. This places a significant responsibility on practitioners to self-regulate.

The development of any ADR system proceeds on the basis of how well it meets its goals. There should be multiple criteria in measuring the success of any program. In some systems, mediation success is measured by the number of cases settled. This is inappropriate. Mediation offers significant benefits other than settlement, which must be considered in evaluating success.

Regarding policy/ethical issues, there is strong sentiment that some classes of cases should be excluded from ADR or a particular process. Domestic violence and sexual harassment grievances are among those considered for exclusion. Other practitioners, however, maintain it is mistaken to exclude such entire classes of cases.

A neutral requires training in the process in which she is going to practice, e.g., mediation, arbitration, etc. This will familiarize her with the rules and attributes of the process, as well as aid in developing the skills required. Such training, of varying depth, is available from a number of sources. Whether a neutral needs subject matter knowledge (and therefore special training or education) to serve effectively is a more difficult issue. While not required in most cases, such knowledge may be expected by the parties and may help to enrich the neutral's abilities. This varies with the process and the subject matter of the conflict. Theoretical knowledge regarding the process can also enhance the mediator's abilities.

Neutrals are faced with ethical dilemmas on an ongoing basis. The SPIDR Standards require the neutral to act in good faith and serve impartially. Neutrals must provide disputants with sufficient information about the process so that the participants can give informed consent to participate. Neutrals must protect confidentiality and avoid conflicts of interest. Finally, they must be prompt and make sure the parties are aware of the consequences of their agreements.

While these practice guidelines may appear easy to follow, they are not. In order to be internalized, they should be read in conjunction with factual studies giving rise to ethical dilemmas.

Neutrals are also responsible for ensuring that the interests of those not represented at the meeting are kept in mind. Further, a neutral must not participate in a case that she is not competent to handle. Finally, a mediator must safeguard the autonomy and self-determination of the parties. This is a complex and serious responsibility.

A neutral is ethically bound to maintain the integrity of the process through aid to new neutrals, education of the public about the process, and control of the process. A neutral must stay within the boundaries of her role as an arbitrator or mediator. Finally, advertising by a neutral must be honest and her fees must be disclosed to the parties.

A common practice issue in mediation is who can be present and participate. While this decision may depend on local practice in the field, the needs of the parties should be the neutral's first consideration.

EXERCISES

1. Write a brief paper explaining why ethical standards are essential in any profession.

2. Research your jurisdiction and describe each court-annexed or court-referred ADR program. Determine which processes are used, who serves as neutral, how the program is funded, and how decisions are appealed.

3. Interview a neutral in a court-annexed ADR program and a private neutral. Obtain their opinions on institutionalizing ADR within the court system.

4. Interview a judge, an attorney, and a litigant, each of whom is familiar with or has been through a court-annexed or court-referred ADR process. Determine whether they like or dislike the process and why.

5. Research and discuss five legal issues that went to trial and resulted in new common law being made in the last five years.

6. Determine what the status of regulation or licensure of ADR providers is in your jurisdiction. Is it being discussed or planned?

7. Determine what evaluative processes are being used in your jurisdiction's court-annexed programs.

8. In your jurisdiction, determine which types of cases are excluded from ADR and which groups or constituencies participated in the decision to exclude them and their rationale for their position.

9. Check your state's court rules to determine what training requirements are listed for ADR providers. Is there any subject matter expertise required? Are there higher requirements for custody mediators? Compare your state's training requirements with those of a neighboring state.

10. Read and discuss in class the examples provided in SPIDR, *Making the Tough Calls: Ethical Exercises for Neutral Dispute Resolvers,* and Robert A. Baruch Bush, *The Dilemmas of Mediation Practice: A Study of Ethical Dilemmas and Policy Implications.*

Appendix A

Standards of Conduct for Mediators

Introductory Note

The initiative for these standards came from three professional groups: the American Arbitration Association, the American Bar Association, and the Society of Professionals in Dispute Resolution. The purpose of this initiative was to develop a set of standards to serve as a general framework for the practice of mediation. The effort is a step in the development of the field and a tool to assist practitioners in it — a beginning, not an end. The standards are intended to apply to all types of mediation. It is recognized, however, that in some cases the application of these standards may be affected by laws or contractual agreements.

Preface

The standards of conduct for mediators are intended to perform three major functions: to serve as a guide for the conduct of mediators; to inform the mediating parties; and to promote public confidence in mediation as a process for resolving disputes. The standards draw on existing codes of conduct for mediators and take into account issues and problems that have surfaced in mediation practice. They are offered in the hope that they will serve an educational function and provide assistance to individuals, organizations, and institutions involved in mediation.

155

Mediation is a process in which an impartial third party — a mediator — facilitates the resolution of a dispute by promoting voluntary agreement (or "self-determination") by the parties to the dispute. A mediator facilitates communication, promotes understanding, focuses the parties on their interests, and seeks creative problem solving to enable the parties to reach their own agreement. These standards give meaning to this definition of mediation.

I. Self-Determination: A Mediator Shall Recognize that Mediation Is Based on the Principle of Self-Determination by the Parties.

Self-determination is the fundamental principle of mediation. It requires that the mediation process rely upon the ability of the parties to reach a voluntary, uncoerced agreement. Any party may withdraw from mediation at any time.

COMMENTS

- The mediator may provide information about the process, raise issues, and help parties explore options. The primary role of the mediator is to facilitate a voluntary resolution of a dispute. Parties shall be given the opportunity to consider all proposed options.
- A mediator cannot personally ensure that each party has made a fully informed choice to reach a particular agreement, but it is a good practice for the mediator to make the parties aware of the importance of consulting other professionals, where appropriate, to help them make informed decisions.

II. Impartiality: A Mediator Shall Conduct the Mediation in an Impartial Manner.

The concept of mediator impartiality is central to the mediation process. A mediator shall mediate only those matters in which she or he can remain impartial and evenhanded. If at any time the mediator is unable to conduct the process in an impartial manner, the mediator is obligated to withdraw.

COMMENTS

- A mediator shall avoid conduct that gives the appearance of partiality toward one of the parties. The quality of the mediation process is enhanced when the parties have confidence in the impartiality of the mediator.
- When mediators are appointed by a court or institution, the appointing agency has an obligation to ensure that mediators serve impartially.
- A mediator should guard against partiality or prejudice based on race, color, creed, national origin, age, sex, and sexual orientation.

III. Conflicts of Interest: A Mediator Shall Disclose all Actual and Potential Conflicts of Interest Reasonably Known to the Mediator. After Disclosure, the Mediator Shall Decline to Mediate Unless all Parties Choose to Retain the Mediator. The Need to Protect Against Conflict of Interest Also Governs Conduct that Occurs During and After the Mediation.

A conflict of interest is a dealing or relationship that might create an impression of possible bias. The basic approach to questions of conflict of interest is consistent with the concept of self-determination. The mediator has a responsibility to disclose all actual and potential conflicts that are reasonably known to the mediator and could reasonably be seen as raising a question about impartiality. If all parties agree to mediate after being informed of conflicts, the mediator may proceed with the mediation. If, however, the conflict of interest casts serious doubt on the integrity of the process, the mediator shall decline to proceed.

A mediator must avoid the appearance of conflict of interest both during and after the mediation. Without the consent of all parties, a mediator shall not subsequently establish a professional relationship with one of the parties in a related matter, or in an unrelated matter under circumstances which would raise legitimate questions about the integrity of the mediation process.

COMMENTS

- A mediator shall avoid conflict of interest in recommending the services of other professionals. A mediator may make reference to professional referral services or associations which maintain rosters of qualified professionals.
- Potential conflict of interest may arise between administrators of mediation programs and mediators and there may be strong pressures on the mediator to settle a particular case or cases. The mediator's commitment must be to the parties and the process. Pressures from outside of the mediation process should never influence the mediator to coerce parties to settle.

IV. Competence: A Mediator Shall Mediate Only When the Mediator Has the Necessary Qualifications to Satisfy the Reasonable Expectations of the Parties.

Any person may be selected as a mediator, provided that the parties are satisfied with the mediator's qualifications. Training and experience in mediation, however, are often necessary for effective mediation. A person who offers herself or himself as available to serve as a mediator gives parties and the public the expectation that she or he has the competency to mediate effectively. In court-connected or other forms of mandated mediation, it is essential that mediators assigned to the parties have the requisite training and experience.

COMMENTS

- Mediators should have information available for the parties regarding their relevant training, education, and experience.
- The requirements for appearing on a list of mediators must be made public and available to interested persons.
- When mediators are appointed by a court or institution, the appointing agency shall make reasonable efforts to ensure that each mediator is qualified for the particular mediation.

V. Confidentiality: A Mediator Shall Maintain the Reasonable Expectations of the Parties with Regard to Confidentiality.

The reasonable expectations of the parties with regard to confidentiality shall be met by the mediator. The parties' expectations of confidentiality depend on the circumstances of the mediation and any agreements they may make. The mediator shall not disclose any matter that a party expects to be confidential unless given permission by all parties or unless required by law or other public policy.

COMMENTS

- The parties may make their own rules with respect to confidentiality, or the accepted practice of an individual mediator or institution may dictate a particular set of expectations. Since the parties' expectations regarding confidentiality are important, the mediator should discuss these expectations with the parties.
- If the mediator holds private sessions with a party, the nature of these sessions with regard to confidentiality should be discussed prior to undertaking such sessions.
- In order to protect the integrity of the mediation, a mediator should avoid communicating information about how the parties acted in the

mediation process, the merits of the case, or settlement offers. The mediator may report, if required, whether parties appeared at a scheduled mediation.

- Where the parties have agreed that all or a portion of the information disclosed during a mediation is confidential, the parties' agreement should be respected by the mediator.
- Confidentiality should not be construed to limit or prohibit the effective monitoring, research, or evaluation of mediation programs by responsible persons. Under appropriate circumstances, researchers may be permitted to obtain access to statistical data and, with the permission of the parties, to individual case files, observations of live mediations, and interviews with participants.

VI. Quality of the Process: A Mediator Shall Conduct the Mediation Fairly, Diligently, and in a Manner Consistent with the Principle of Self-Determination by the Parties.

A mediator shall work to ensure a quality process and to encourage mutual respect among the parties. A quality process requires a commitment by the mediator to diligence and procedural fairness. There should be adequate opportunity for each party in the mediation to participate in the discussions. The parties decide when and under what conditions they will reach an agreement or terminate a mediation.

COMMENTS

- A mediator may agree to mediate only when he or she is prepared to commit the attention essential to an effective mediation.
- Mediators should only accept cases when they can satisfy the reasonable expectations of the parties concerning the timing of the process. A mediator should not allow a mediation to be unduly delayed by the parties or their representatives.
- The presence or absence of persons at a mediation depends on the agreement of the parties and mediator. The parties and mediator

may agree that others may be excluded from particular sessions or from the entire mediation process.

- The primary purpose of a mediator is to facilitate the parties' voluntary agreement. This role differs substantially from other professional-client relationships. Mixing the role of a mediator and the role of a professional advising a client is problematic, and mediators must strive to distinguish between the roles. A mediator should, therefore, refrain from providing professional advice. Where appropriate, a mediator should recommend that parties seek outside professional advice, or consider resolving their dispute through arbitration, counseling, neutral evaluation, or other processes. A mediator who undertakes, at the request of the parties, an additional dispute resolution role in the same matter assumes increased responsibilities and obligations that may be governed by the standards of other professions.
- A mediator shall withdraw from a mediation when incapable of serving or when unable to remain impartial.
- A mediator shall withdraw from mediation or postpone a session if the mediation is being used to further illegal conduct, or if a party is unable to participate due to drug, alcohol, or other physical or mental incapacity.
- Mediators should not permit their behavior in the mediation process to be guided by a desire for a high settlement rate.

VII.   Advertising and Solicitation: A Mediator Shall Be Truthful in Advertising and Solicitation for Mediation.

Advertising or any other communication with the public concerning services offered or regarding the education, training, and expertise of the mediator shall be truthful. Mediators shall refrain from promises and guarantees of results.

COMMENTS

- It is imperative that communication with the public educate and instill confidence in the process.

161

- In an advertisement or other communication to the public, a mediator may make reference to meeting state, national, or private organization qualifications only if the entity referred to has a procedure for qualifying mediators and the mediator has been duly granted the requisite status.

VIII.   Fees: A Mediator Shall Fully Disclose and Explain the Basis of Compensation, Fees, and Charges to the Parties.

The parties should be provided sufficient information about fees at the outset of a mediation to determine if they wish to retain the services of a mediator. If a mediator charges fees, the fees shall be reasonable, considering, among other things, the mediation service, the type and complexity of the matter, the expertise of the mediator, the time required, and the rates customary in the community. The better practice in reaching an understanding about fees is to set down the arrangements in a written agreement.

COMMENTS

- A mediator who withdraws from a mediation should return any unearned fee to the parties.
- A mediator should not enter into a fee agreement which is contingent upon the result of the mediation or amount of the settlement.
- Co-mediators who share a fee should hold to standards of reasonableness in determining the allocation of fees.
- A mediator should not accept a fee for referral of a matter to another mediator or to any other person.

IX. Obligations to the Mediation Process: Mediators Have a Duty to Improve the Practice of Mediation.

COMMENTS

- Mediators are regarded as knowledgeable in the process of mediation. They have an obligation to use their knowledge to help educate the public about mediation; to make mediation accessible to those who would like to use it; to correct abuses; and to improve their professional skills and abilities.

Appendix B

Code of Ethics for Arbitrators in Commercial Disputes*

Preamble

The use of commercial arbitration to resolve a wide variety of disputes has grown extensively and forms a significant part of the system of justice on which our society relies for fair determination of legal rights. Persons who act as commercial arbitrators therefore undertake serious responsibilities to the public as well as to the parties. Those responsibilities include important ethical obligations.

Few cases of unethical behavior by commercial arbitrators have arisen. Nevertheless, the American Bar Association and the American Arbitration Association believe that it is in the public interest to set forth generally accepted standards of ethical conduct for guidance of arbitrators and parties in commercial disputes. By establishing this code, the sponsors hope to contribute to the maintenance of high standards and continued confidence in the process of arbitration.

There are many different types of commercial arbitration. Some cases are conducted under arbitration rules established by various organizations and trade associations, while others are conducted without such rules. Although most cases are arbitrated pursuant to voluntary agreement of the parties, certain types of dispute are submitted to arbitration by reason of particular laws. This code is intended to apply to all

*American Arbitration Association and the American Bar Association, 1977

such proceedings in which dispute or claims are submitted for decision to one or more arbitrators appointed in a manner provided by an agreement of the parties, by applicable arbitration rules, or by law. In all such cases, the persons who have the power to decide should observe fundamental standards of ethical conduct. In this code all such persons are called "arbitrators" although, in some types of cases, they might be called "umpires" or have some other title.

Various aspects of the conduct of arbitrators, including some matters covered by the code, may be governed by agreements of the parties, by arbitration rules to which the parties have agreed, or by applicable law. This code does not take the place of nor supersede such agreements, rules, or laws and does not establish new or additional grounds for judicial review of arbitration awards.

While this code is intended to provide ethical guidelines in many types of arbitration, it does not form a part of the arbitration rules of the American Arbitration Association or of any other organization, nor is it intended to apply to mediation or conciliation. Labor arbitration is governed by the Code of Professional Responsibility for Arbitrators of Labor-Management Disputes, not by this code.

Arbitrators, like judges, have the power to decide cases. However, unlike full-time judges, arbitrators are usually engaged in other occupations before, during, and after the time that they serve as arbitrators. Often, arbitrators are purposely chosen from the same trade or industry as the parties in order to bring special knowledge to the task of deciding. This code recognizes these fundamental differences between arbitrators and judges.

In some types of arbitration, there are three or more arbitrators. In such cases, it is sometimes the practice for each party, acting alone, to appoint one arbitrator and for the other arbitrators to be designated by those two, by the parties, or by an independent institution or individual. The sponsors of this code believe that it is preferable for parties to agree that all arbitrators should comply with the same ethical standards. However, it is recognized that there is a long-established practice in some types of arbitration for the arbitrators who are appointed by one party, acting alone, to be governed by special ethical considerations. Those special considerations are set forth in the last section of the code, headed "Ethical Considerations Relating to Arbitrators Appointed by One Party."

Although this code is sponsored by the American Arbitration Association and the American Bar Association, its use is not limited to arbitrations administered by the AAA or to cases in which the arbitrators are lawyers. Rather, it is presented as a public service to provide guidance in all types of commercial arbitration.

Canon I. An Arbitrator Should Uphold the Integrity and Fairness of the Arbitration Processes

A. Fair and just processes for resolving dispute are indispensable in our society. Commercial arbitration is an important method for deciding many types of disputes. In order for commercial arbitration to be effective, there must be broad public confidence in the integrity and fairness of the process. Therefore, an arbitrator has a responsibility not only to the parties but also the process of arbitration itself, and must observe high standards of conduct so that the integrity and fairness of the process will be preserved. Accordingly, an arbitrator should recognize a responsibility to the public, to the parties whose rights will be decided, and to all other participants in the proceeding. The provisions of this code should be construed and applied to further these objectives.

B. It is inconsistent with the integrity of the arbitration process for persons to solicit appointment for themselves. However, a person may indicate a general willingness to serve as an arbitrator.

C. Persons should accept appointment as arbitrators only if they believe that they can be available to conduct the arbitration promptly.

D. After accepting appointment and while serving as an arbitrator, a person should avoid entering into any financial, business, professional, family or social relationship, or acquiring any financial or personal interest, which is likely to affect impartiality or which might reasonably create the appearance of partiality or bias. For a reasonable period of time after the decision of a case, persons who have served as arbitrators should avoid entering into any such relationship, or acquiring any such interest, in circumstances which might reasonably create the appearance that they had been influenced in the arbitration by the anticipation or expectation of the relationship or interest.

E. Arbitrators should conduct themselves in a way that is fair to all parties and should not be swayed by outside pressure, by public clamor, by fear of criticism, or by self interest.

F. When an arbitrator's authority is derived from an agreement of the parties, the arbitrator should neither exceed that authority nor do less than is required to exercise that authority completely. Where the agreement of the parties sets forth procedures to be followed in conducting the arbitration or refers to rules to be followed, it is the obligation of the arbitrator to comply with such procedures or rules.

G. An arbitrator should make all reasonable efforts to prevent delaying tactics, harassment of parties or other participants, or other abuse or disruption of the arbitration process.

H. The ethical obligations of an arbitrator begin upon acceptance of the appointment and continue throughout all stages of the proceeding. In addition, wherever specifically set forth in this code, certain ethical obligations begin as soon as a person is requested to serve as an arbitrator and certain ethical obligations continue even after the decision in the case has been given to the parties.

Canon II. An Arbitrator Should Disclose Any Interest or Relationship Likely to Affect Impartiality or Which Might Create an Appearance of Partiality or Bias

Introductory Note

This code reflects the prevailing principle that arbitrators should disclose the existence of interests or relationships that are likely to affect their impartiality or that might reasonably create an appearance that they are biased against one party or favorable to another. These provisions of the code are intended to be applied realistically so that the burden of detailed disclosure does not become so great that it is impractical for persons in the business world to be arbitrators, thereby depriving parties of the services of those who might be best informed and qualified to decide particular types of cases.

This code does not limit the freedom of parties to agree on whomever they choose as an arbitrator. When parties, with knowledge of a person's interests and relationships, nevertheless desire that individual to serve as an arbitrator, that person may properly serve.

Disclosure

A. Persons who are requested to serve as arbitrators should, before accepting, disclose

(1) any direct or indirect financial or personal interest in the outcome of the arbitration;

(2) any existing or past financial, business, professional, family or social relationships which are likely to affect impartiality or which
might reasonably create an appearance of partiality or bias.

Persons requested to serve as arbitrators should disclose any such relationships which they personally have with any party or its lawyer, or
with any individual whom they have been told will be a witness.
They should also disclose any such relationships involving members
of their families or their current employers, partners or business asso-
ciates.

B. Persons who are requested to accept appointment as arbitrators
should make a reasonable effort to inform themselves of any interests
or relationships described in the preceding paragraph A.

C. The obligation to disclose interests or relationships described in the
preceding paragraph A is a continuing duty which requires a person
who accepts appointment as an arbitrator to disclose, at any stage of
the arbitration, any such interests or relationships which may arise, or
which are recalled or discovered.

D. Disclosure should be made to all parties unless other procedures for
disclosure are provided in the rules or practices of an institution
which is administering the arbitration. Where more than one arbitrator has been appointed, each should inform the others of the interests and relationships which have been disclosed.

E. In the event that an arbitrator is requested by all parties to withdraw,
the arbitrator should do so. In the event that an arbitrator is requested
to withdraw by less than all of the parties because of alleged partiality or bias, the arbitrator should withdraw unless either of the following circumstances exists.

(1) If an agreement of the parties, or arbitration rules agreed to by
the parties, establishes procedures for determining challenges to
arbitrators, then those procedures should be followed; or,

(2) if the arbitrator, after carefully considering the matter, determines that the reason for the challenge is not substantial, and
that he or she can nevertheless act and decide the case impartially and fairly, and that withdrawal would cause unfair delay or
expense to another party or would be contrary to the ends of
justice.

Canon III. An Arbitrator in Communicating with the Parties Should Avoid Impropriety or the Appearance of Impropriety

A. If an agreement of the parties, or applicable arbitration rules referred to in that agreement, establishes the manner or content of communications between the arbitrator and the parties, the arbitrator should follow those procedures notwithstanding any contrary provision of the following paragraphs B and C.

B. Unless otherwise provided in applicable arbitration rules or in an agreement of the parties, arbitrators should not discuss a case with any party in the absence of each other party, except in any of the following circumstances.

   (1) Discussions may be had with a party concerning such matters as setting the time and place of hearings or making other arrangements for the conduct of the proceedings. However, the arbitrator should promptly inform each other party of the discussion and should not make any final determination concerning the matter discussed before giving each absent party an opportunity to express its views.

   (2) If a party fails to be present at a hearing after having been given due notice, the arbitrator may discuss the case with any party who is present.

   (3) If all parties request or consent to it, such discussion may take place.

C. Unless otherwise provided in applicable arbitration rules or in an agreement of the parties, whenever an arbitrator communicates in writing with one party, the arbitrator should at the same time send a copy of the communication to each other party. Whenever the arbitrator receives any written communication concerning the case from one party which has not already been sent to each other party, the arbitrator should do so.

Canon IV. An Arbitrator Should Conduct the Proceedings Fairly and Diligently

A. An arbitrator should conduct the proceedings in an evenhanded manner and treat all parties with equality and fairness at all stages of the proceedings.

B. An arbitrator should perform duties diligently and conclude the case as promptly as the circumstances reasonably permit.

C. An arbitrator should be patient and courteous to the parties, to their lawyers, and to the witnesses, and should encourage similar conduct by all participants in the proceedings.

D. Unless otherwise agreed by the parties or provided in arbitration rules agreed to by the parties, an arbitrator should accord to all parties the right to appear in person and to be heard after due notice of the time and place of hearing.

E. An arbitrator should not deny any party the opportunity to be represented by counsel.

F. If a party fails to appear after due notice, an arbitrator should proceed with the arbitration when authorized to do so by the agreement of the parties, the rules agreed to by the parties, or by the law. However, an arbitrator should do so only after receiving assurances that notice has been given to the absent party.

G. When an arbitrator determines that more information than has been presented by the parties is required to decide the case, it is not improper for the arbitrator to ask questions, call witnesses, and request documents or other evidence.

H. It is not improper for an arbitrator to suggest to the parties that they discuss the possibility of settlement of the case. However, an arbitrator should not be present or otherwise participate in the settlement discussions unless requested to do so by all parties. An arbitrator should not exert pressure on any party to settle.

I. Nothing in this code is intended to prevent a person from acting as a mediator or conciliator of a dispute in which he or she has been appointed as arbitrator, if requested to do so by all parties or where authorized or required to do so by applicable laws or rules.

J. When there is more than one arbitrator, the arbitrators should afford each other the full opportunity to participate in all aspects of the proceedings.

Canon V. An Arbitrator Should Make Decisions in a Just, Independent, and Deliberate Manner

A. An arbitrator should, after careful deliberation, decide all issues submitted for determination. An arbitrator should decide no other issues.
B. An arbitrator should decide all matters justly, exercising independent judgment, and should not permit outside pressure to affect the decision.
C. An arbitrator should not delegate the duty to decide to any other person.
D. In the event that all parties agree upon a settlement of issues in dispute and request an arbitrator to embody that agreement in an award, an arbitrator may do so, but is not required to do so unless satisfied with the propriety of the terms of settlement. Whenever an arbitrator embodies a settlement by the parties in an award, the arbitrator should state in the award that it is based on an agreement of the parties.

Canon VI. An Arbitrator Should Be Faithful to the Relationship of Trust and Confidentiality Inherent in That Office

A. An arbitrator is in a relationship of trust to the parties and should not, at any time, use confidential information acquired during the arbitration proceeding to gain personal advantage or advantage for others, or to affect adversely the interest of another.
B. Unless otherwise agreed by the parties, or required by applicable rules or law, an arbitrator should keep confidential all matters relating to the arbitration proceedings and decision.
C. It is not proper at any time for an arbitrator to inform anyone of the decision in advance of the time it is given to all parties. In a case in which there is more than one arbitrator, it is not proper at any time for an arbitrator to inform anyone concerning the deliberations of the arbitrators. After an arbitration award has been made, it is not proper for an arbitrator to assist in postarbitral proceedings, except as is required by law.

D. In many types of arbitration it is customary practice for the arbitrators to serve without pay. However, in some types of cases it is customary for arbitrators to receive compensation for their services and reimbursement for their expenses. In cases in which any such payments are made, all persons who are requested to serve, or who are serving as arbitrators, should be governed by the same high standards of integrity and fairness as apply to their other activities in the case. Accordingly, such persons should scrupulously avoid bargaining with parties over the amount of payments or engaging in any communications concerning payments which would create an appearance of coercion or other impropriety. In the absence of governing provisions in the agreement of the parties or in rules agreed to by the parties or in applicable law, certain practices relating to payments are generally recognized as being preferable in order to preserve the integrity and fairness of the arbitration process. These practices include the following.

(1) It is preferable that before the arbitrator finally accepts appointment the basis of payment be established and that all parties be informed thereof in writing.

(2) In cases conducted under the rules or administration of an institution that is available to assist in making arrangements for payments, the payments should be arranged by the institution to avoid the necessity for communication by the arbitrators directly with the parties concerning the subject.

(3) In cases where no institution is available to assist in making arrangement for payments, it is preferable that any discussions with arbitrators concerning payments should take place in the presence of all parties.

Canon VII. Ethical Considerations Relating to Arbitrators Appointed by One Party

Introductory Note

In some types of arbitration in which there are three arbitrators, it is customary for each party, acting alone, to appoint one arbitrator. The third arbitrator is then appointed by agreement either of the parties or of the two arbitrators, or, failing such agreement, by an independent institution or individual. In some of these types of arbitration, all three arbitrators are customarily considered to be neutral and are expected to observe the same standards of ethical conduct. However, there are also many types of tripartite arbitration in which it has been the practice that the two arbitrators appointed by the parties are not considered to be neutral and are expected to observe many — but not all — of the same ethical standards as the neutral third arbitrator. For the purposes of this code, an arbitrator appointed by one party who is not expected to observe all of the same standards as the third arbitrator is called a "nonneutral arbitrator." [Canon VII goes on to describe the ethical obligations that nonneutral party-appointed arbitrators should observe and those that are not applicable to them.]

Appendix C

Example of Med-Arb*

John Cotesworth, Evan Handy, and Cynthia Paul attended veterinary school together in the mid-1960s. During school they were best friends and decided to go into partnership together in a small town in the mid-west when they graduated. Because they were such close friends they decided to run their practice on a very informal basis. They each contributed money to buy equipment and supplies, rent a clinic, and advertise their services. Handy's father had been a veterinarian and gave them a lot of good advice, some equipment, and his patient list when he retired. Cotesworth, Handy, and Paul agreed to share profits equally.

For almost 15 years the practice went quite smoothly. The clinic developed an excellent reputation in the community and each of the veterinarians was highly respected and well known. Paul served three terms as mayor, Cotesworth was active in United Way, and Handy was named Citizen of the Year in 1984 for his work with senior citizens.

In May 1986, the three started to have problems. Cotesworth and his wife were divorced after several months of a child custody battle. Cotesworth's ex-wife remained Cynthia Paul's best friend, and Paul found it increasingly hard to work with Cotesworth given what his former wife told her about him. Handy, who had always been a social drinker, began occasionally to show up for work intoxicated or hung over and sometimes was unable to perform even routine surgeries. Cotesworth had no patience with Handy's drinking and would refuse to speak to Handy for several days.

Soon these personal problems started having professional ramifications. Cotesworth felt that because he was single, Paul and Handy expected him to do most of the weekend emergency work but were unwilling to compensate him for it. Paul felt that both Cotesworth and Handy assigned the particularly sensitive cases to her because of her diplomacy with people and her ability to calm nervous animals. By mid-

*Taken from Susan M. Leeson & Bryan M. Johnston, Ending It: Dispute Resolution in America 151-153 (1988).

year the three veterinarians could barely speak to one another and realized that they should stop trying to work together.

Every time Cotesworth, Handy, and Paul tried to discuss the best way to end their partnership they got into serious arguments. None was content with a three-way split. Paul and Cotesworth felt they had contributed much more than their share of time to the practice, while Handy contended they should not be allowed to benefit from all the help they had received from his father when they were starting their practice. Neither Cotesworth nor Paul wanted to stop practicing veterinary medicine, although Handy readily admitted that he was ready for a career change. Both Cotesworth and Paul wanted the equipment and the clinic; Handy said he would rather sell his share to anybody else than Cotesworth and Paul.

Cotesworth finally consulted his lawyer about the best way to dissolve the partnership. His attorney asked to see a copy of the original partnership agreement in order to study the provisions for dissolution. Cotesworth explained that when the three had started out they were best friends and that they had operated all these years without a partnership agreement. Cotesworth's lawyer listened to her client's explanation of the problem confronting the veterinarians and explained med-arb. The three could try to negotiate a settlement to their dispute with the aid of a neutral mediator. Lacking agreement, the mediator either could offer an opinion or could turn the dispute over to an arbitrator. Cotesworth's lawyer gave him a list of three people in the community who practice mediation.

Cotesworth, Handy, and Paul interviewed the three mediators and agreed that one would be acceptable. They also agreed that they did not want everyone in the town to know about their problems and concluded that the mediator should be authorized to arbitrate the dispute if they were unable to resolve their dispute. When they met, the mediator spent several hours with the three explaining mediation and establishing ground rules. Achieving agreement on a process was a big step. In addition to agreeing on a process, they agreed to meet twice a week for two hours until they either came to agreement or reached stalemate.

The three veterinarians stayed in mediation for almost five weeks. Sometimes they met together, sometimes the mediator met with them individually or in pairs. The mediator was able to get them to talk about what had happened to their friendship as well as the best way to dissolve the partnership. Cotesworth finally understood that Paul had been angry with him because of his divorce and comments from his ex-wife. He had thought she disapproved of the way he had handled a case several months ago and was holding a grudge. Cotesworth and Paul both came to a better understanding of Handy's drinking problem, apparently precipitated by the fact that he no longer liked veterinary medicine but thought he was too old to make a career change. Cotesworth and Handy listened to Paul's resentment about being given the most difficult patients. All were able to acknowledge how important their friendship had been over the years.

Through mediation Cotesworth and Paul were able to agree that they both wanted to continue to practice veterinary medicine in the same town and that they did not want to be in competition with one another. They knew, however, that they would never be close friends as they once had been. They agreed to retain a lawyer to draw up a formal partnership agreement.

Despite their progress in mediation, the three were not able to agree how much Handy should be paid for his share of the partnership. That issue eventually was turned over to the mediator, now arbitrator, for a decision. Cotesworth and Paul then agreed on what percentage of the award each of them should pay Handy. Handy used his share of the settlement to relocate in another community to work with a group of cattle breeders.

Appendix D

Recommendations for Mandatory Mediation

The following are Recommendations promulgated by the Society for Professionals in Dispute Resolution in 1991 as part of Report #1 of the Law and Public Policy Committee of the Society of Professionals in Dispute Resolution, Mandated Participation and Settlement Coercion: Dispute Resolution as It Relates to the Courts.

1. Mandating participation in non-binding dispute resolution processes often is appropriate. However, compulsory programs should be carefully designed to reflect a variety of important concerns. These concerns include the monetary and emotional costs for the parties, as well as the interests of the parties in achieving results that suit their needs and will last; the justice system's ability to deliver results that do not harm the interest of those groups that have historically operated at a disadvantage in this society; the need to have courts that function efficiently and effectively; the importance of the public's trust in the justice system; the interests of non-parties whose lives are affected and sometimes disrupted by litigation; the importance of the court's development of legal precedent; and the general interest in maximizing party choice. In weighing these valid and sometimes competing concerns, policy makers should be cautious not to give undue emphasis to the desire to facilitate the efficient administration of court business and thereby subordinate other interests. Participation should be mandated only when the compulsory program is more likely to serve these broad interests of the parties, the justice system, and the public than would procedures that would be used absent mandatory dispute resolution.

Possible Positive Effects of Mandated Participation

Several arguments favor mandated participation in dispute resolution interests:

a. The parties frequently respond favorably to mandated dispute resolution. Some are receptive to court control of the procedures. In some instances, this is preferable to placing control in the hands of an opponent, who may be forcing them to spend thousands of dollars in litigation while refusing a "face-to-face" discussion.

b. Rates of voluntary usage are often low, perhaps because parties or their lawyers may be more accustomed to the litigation process or do not want to signal to their adversary a desire for compromise. Mandating use of dispute resolution processes often increases substantially the total number of cases settled through their use. As a result, more parties arrive at solutions that they prefer to an adjudicated result and that better suit their needs and preferences than would a court-imposed judgment. Moreover, the settlements may reduce disruption caused by protracted litigation in the lives of affected nonparties, such as the children of a divorcing couple. These settlements, particularly those that avert trials and post-judgment motions, may also free court resources for other cases.

c. Effective dispute resolution programs require adequate administrative support. By increasing the caseload, mandated participation allows the administration to be provided on a cost-effective basis.

d. The expanded use of these processes as a result of mandating participation will serve to educate the parties and their lawyers, perhaps resulting in an increased voluntary use of dispute resolution programs outside the court processes.

Possible Negative Effects of Mandated Participation

The Committee also notes several possible negative effects:

a. If not designed and administered well, mandated processes may simply pose an unnecessary and costly hurdle for parties who will resolve their case by trial or settlement in any event.

b. There is a risk that the flexibility and high quality of dispute resolution programs will fall prey to the deadly routinizing influence of bureaucracy. In mediation programs particularly, narrowly focused procedures and briefer, more formulaic sessions seem likely to resolve a narrower range of issues and thus not meet the broader needs of the parties. The short, rigid sessions may result in lower party involvement, poor resolution, and thus lower voluntary compliance with the resolution.

c. Broadly mandated participation may sweep cases into an inappropriate process, resulting in wasted time and effort, unfair settlements, and other possible harm.

d. The parties may have preferences for particular procedures. For example, the more structured presentation of the case at trial or arbitration may be more comfortable than negotiation processes for parties who are fearful of each other.

The Effects of Coercion to Settle

If there is coercion to settle within the process, this shifts the weights and counterweights relevant to determining whether participation should be mandated. A party's option to decline settlement provides the primary protection for the fairness of the process. In addition, the freely obtained consent by the parties makes it more likely that their interests will be served by the settlement and that they will voluntarily comply with it. Coercion to settle within mandatory processes may remove, as a practical matter, this option to forego settlement. Further, the coercion may affect the procedural fairness by increasing the degree to which access to trial depends on wealth.

Balancing Competing Possibilities

Mandatory dispute resolution could either improve or impede the administration of justice. This uncertainty counsels for careful consideration before a compulsory program is instituted and careful monitoring as it is administered. At a minimum, participation should be compulsory only when Recommendations 2, 3, and 4, regarding funding, coercion to settle, and quality, are met.

2. Funding for mandatory dispute resolution programs should be provided on a basis comparable to funding for trials.

Mandatory dispute resolution has the same compulsory character as hearings and trials, so the public commitment to provide litigation fa-

179

cilities without charging the users except through the imposition of a filing fee and allocation of court costs should be expanded to provide access to mandatory dispute resolution processes on a comparable basis.

User fees imposed only on those referred to mandatory processes pose particular problems. If not properly regulated, dispute resolution user fees can result in undesirable coercion to settle for the parties who cannot afford them and in unseemly practices through which the court provides lucrative employment to private providers.

Under current practices, in exceptional cases the parties must pay substantial litigation user fees which greatly exceed the filing fee. For example, the court may appoint a special master to hold an evidentiary hearing and impose the expense on the parties. In these exceptional cases, the courts may also properly impose substantial dispute resolution fees on the parties. However, the court should first determine that the burden is not unreasonable given the amount at stake and financial abilities of the parties.

Except in these unusual cases, parties who are ordered to use a process should not also be ordered to pay the cost. User fees should never be charged in criminal cases, where access to justice is particularly important.

The structure of public funding for mandatory processes may also affect quality. For example, if payments are based on the numbers of dispositions, the neutrals may have an incentive to settle without regard to informing weaker parties of their rights.

When the third-party will receive a substantial fee, either from the court or from the parties who are mandated to use the process, referral should not be made to a particular individual except in unusual circumstances. Instead, the parties typically should be permitted to choose from a panel of qualified persons and should be told the qualifications of the panel members. Fees for mandatory programs should be set by the court.

3. Coercion to settle in the form of reports to the trier of fact and of financial disincentives to trial should not be used in connection with mandated mediation. In connection with court-annexed arbitration, the financial disincentives should be clear, commensurate with the interests at stake, and used only when the parties could afford to risk their imposition and proceed to trial.

Financial disincentives to trial and reports on substantive issues to the trier of fact are sometimes imposed to make the parties take the process more seriously and to "think twice" before proceeding to trial.

In essence, these pressures are designed to avoid the problem of parties who refuse to participate meaningfully in the process. The pressures may be applied *ad hoc,* such as when the settlement evaluation is given by the judge who will later hear the case without a jury.

Mediation: Settlement coercion tied to a neural's evaluation has a significant negative impact on mediation. The coercion results in strategic argument by the parties, who accurately view the mediator as having an effect on an adjudicated outcome. Thus, the coercion destroys the environment of frank communication necessary for the negotiation process. Further, the mediator's recommendation seems unlikely to provide the proper basis for judicial resolution or cost shifting, because mediators hold separate meetings with the parties and do not hear evidentiary presentations. For these reasons, financial disincentives to trial and reports to the trier of fact should not be used in connection with mediation.

Hearing Processes: The policy issues regarding pressures to settle are different for hearing processes, such as court-annexed arbitration. The parties already act strategically within the hearing. Moreover, they have the right to present evidence and question adverse witnesses. *Ex parte* conferences with the arbitrators are not permitted. Thus, the prime concerns with financial disincentives following court-annexed arbitration are the effective denial of trial and the disparate effect these disincentives have on those who cannot afford the payments, or even the risk of the payments, and are thus forced to settle.

The wisdom of disincentives in the context of non-binding arbitration depends on the type and level of the disincentive. If the amount is uncertain, such as in shifted attorney's fees for a failure to improve upon the award, few individual parties can afford to take the risk. Further, for fixed-amount disincentives, settlement rates do not seem to be substantially higher when the disincentives are higher. Thus, it would be wise to place a cap on the amount of the disincentive. The amount of the cap should not be so great as to result in a disadvantage based on the relative wealth of the litigants and should not be disproportionate to the value of the case.

It appears unwise to permit transmission of rejected court-annexed arbitration awards to the court or jury. First, the court-annexed arbitration presentations are likely to be summary in nature and the record less comprehensive than in litigation. The court or jury may give the awards undue weight. Second, one purpose of this arbitration is to provide information for settlement negotiations. The procedure will have more credibility as a settlement device if the arbitration award is not transmitted to the court or jury.

4. Mandatory participation should be used only when a high quality program (i) is readily accessible, (ii) permits party participation, (iii) permits lawyer participation when the parties wish it, and (iv) provides clarity about the precise procedures that are being required.

Assuring a high-quality dispute resolution process is of special concern in mandatory programs. The program design should include standards designed to maintain quality. These provisions should be specific and concrete. The provisions will vary considerably by process, but several considerations are key, regardless of the process.

- Persons or programs offering the dispute resolution process should be readily available. This means not only that the parties should be able to use the processes quickly but also that the processes are affordable and easily accessible, and not unduly time-consuming individually or in combination with other court requirements.
- The parties should normally be allowed to attend and participate. (Studies of party satisfaction indicate that their participation and understanding of the process are two of the key advantages of the less formal processes.)
- The parties' lawyers should not be excluded from dispute resolution processes if the parties would like them to be present. Lawyers may act as a crucial check against uninformed and pressured settlements, particularly when they are knowledgeable about the dispute resolution processes. It is the parties in consultation with their lawyers — not public authorities — who are in the best position to decide when the lawyer's presence is indicated. When the parties are unrepresented by counsel, special efforts should be made to make the parties aware of alternatives to settlement and to avoid practices that make them feel that they must settle.
- Race, gender, and ethnic background should not be exclusionary factors in the choice of the neutrals, and the responsibility to use affirmative action to promote ethnic, gender, racial, and cultural diversity is especially great when participation is mandatory.
- It is important to inform parties about the dispute resolution procedures, especially if they are unrepresented. The parties should be told clearly about what they are and are not required to do.
- When the parties are required to attend an assessment conducted by a private practitioner and the purpose is to evaluate the appropriateness of using a dispute resolution process, the courts should maintain oversight. For instance the integrity of the program may be compromised when public officials mandatorily refer the parties for advice

about whether to choose to participate in a dispute resolution process to a private provider who will benefit if the parties elect to participate.

5. Plans for mandated dispute resolution programs should be formed in consultation with judges, other court officials, lawyers, and other dispute resolution professionals as well as representatives of the public. Mandatory programs should be monitored to ensure that they constitute an improvement over existing procedures, using criteria listed in Recommendation 1. The programs should be altered or discontinued when appropriate.

The public authority mandating participation has a special responsibility to ensure that the compulsory program is more likely to serve a variety of public interests (see Recommendation 1) than procedures that would be used absent mandatory dispute resolution. Several planning procedures seem more likely to make this happen.

Expertise has developed on design issues such as timing, choice of case, choice of process and neutral, involvement of lawyers, and fees. Because each of these issues is important, the planning committee for these mandatory programs should include dispute resolution professionals as well as representatives of those affected by the mandated process, such as the court, lawyers, and the public.

A tendency of the courts is to mandate dispute resolution processes that are similar to adjudication. Such processes may not always be appropriate for particular cases. As the dispute resolution field has developed, new procedures have evolved quite rapidly, and subtle but important distinctions among old procedures have come to be understood. For example, in recent years, early evaluation, moderated settlement conferences, mini-trials, and summary jury trials have been pioneered. Further, a significant distinction is emerging between mediation that is open to considering the underlying interests of the parties and meditation that is strictly rights-based. Distinctions among these processes reflect important differences in practice, program, and effect on parties which have substantial implications for training, program, design, and selection of neutrals. Thus, policy-makers, program designers, and judges implementing mandates must be knowledgeable about and sensitive to these variations as they make decisions to mandate participation in dispute resolution procedures.

The design of the program often has unanticipated consequences. For example, setting the mandate after completion of formal discovery may mean that the parties save little, if any, litigation costs even if they settle.

During the early period of a mandatory program, it is especially important that data be collected to determine whether it is meeting the goals set by planners. As part of this process, it is important to examine the effect of the program on such matters as the parties' costs, interests, and satisfaction as well as the effect on court resources. During early stages, data should be gathered to determine whether a substantial number of the participants believe that the mandated participation has been so burdensome as to make it impractical for them to pursue a trial or so injurious to other interests that, in their view, the costs of the mandate outweigh the benefits.

6. Procedures for compulsory referral should include, to the extent feasible, case assessment by a person knowledgeable about dispute resolution procedures and should provide for timely consideration of motions for exclusion.

The program plans should include the development of two kinds of procedures: (1) those to determine when mandates should be used and (2) those permitting timely decisions when a party wishes to opt out.

The choice of appropriate cases and processes is not easily defined and applied by category. Thus, large categorical referrals to a particular process seem likely to result in many parties simply going through the motions, adding to party and court costs. Blanket referrals also seem to result in use of one process rather than a range of processes, so that courts may refer all cases involving, for example, claims below $25,000 to court-annexed arbitration.

Ideally, the mandatory referral system should reduce as much as possible the inclusion of cases for which the dispute resolution process is unlikely to be helpful. In an attempt to avoid imposing unnecessary requirements, many courts are making compulsory referrals on a case-by-case basis, although system needs in high volume programs may result in referral to dispute resolution processes by case category. In any event, in light of imperfect ability to predict when dispute resolution processes will prove helpful, mistakes will be made.

As a result, there should be means to mitigate the consequences of over-broad, especially categorical, mandatory referrals. Any compulsory program should include procedures for exempting cases that are demonstrably inappropriate for the mandatory program, such as when the parties are seeking emergency court relief in cases of spousal abuse. The court should quickly hear motions to be excused which are made on the grounds that the interests of justice would not be served by a mandatory referral. Important considerations in ruling on these motions include the interest of the public in the outcome, the presence of novel issues of law, and the ability of the parties to participate effectively within the process.

Some committee members believe that giving the party a choice of neutrals or process may be another way to mitigate the effects of overbroad mandates. In this report, no recommendation is made on this point. The larger debates about the interplay between public and private providers in dispute resolution will be the focus of the next Law and Public Policy Committee report.

7. Requirements for participation and sanctions for noncompliance should be clearly defined.

Most parties seemed to participate actively in mandated dispute resolution processes even when the statute or rule appears to require no more than mere attendance. In fact, though they vary significantly, settlement rates of about 50 percent are common in mandatory programs. It may not, therefore, be very important to add regulation of participation or strengthen sanctions for those not complying.

Nonetheless, additional clear requirements might be added without being unduly burdensome. Thus, for example, it may be helpful to require attendance by the party as well as the lawyer. When the party is a business entity, it may be useful to require attendance by a party representative with decisionmaking authority. If attendance is burdensome, such a party may be required to be available by telephone. Further, the parties may be required to bring certain information. Where the compliance standards are clear and the sanctions are specified and not unreasonable, the risk of litigation over compliance seems small.

However, requirements for "good faith bargaining" or "meaningful participation," or for the making of offers or concessions, or other substantial and vague provisions seem unwise, on balance. These provisions seem unlikely to have a significant positive effect on behavior, seem likely to prolong the dispute resolution sessions even when the sessions are not productive, and also seem likely to result in satellite litigation over compliance. These contra-indications to vague compliance standards seem more compelling for dispute resolution processes not conducted by a judge or magistrate than for pretrial conferences before a judge or magistrate. If noncompliance occurred in a session that was not conducted by a judge or magistrate, the court must often hold an evidentiary hearing to determine whether a party failed to comply. Thus, efforts to prove noncompliance with vague standards such as "good faith" bargaining or participation are likely to result in an increased demand for testimony by the third-party neutral, presenting a conflict with other public policy favoring confidentiality.

Appendix E

Forms Used in Mediation*

The following forms are provided as examples only. It is strongly recommended that students research local resources to find and develop their own forms.

1. Confidentiality Agreement — only deals with the issue of confidentiality, to be signed before commencing the mediation.
2. Agreement to Mediate — to be signed before commencing the mediation; a fee schedule is usually included.
3. Mediation Retainer Agreement — to be signed before commencing the mediation.
4. Mediation Agreement — contains the final resolution of the parties to a simple dispute.

For forms used in other areas of mediation, see the following:

- *Campus Mediation* — Kathy Domenici, Mediation: Empowerment in Conflict Management (1996).
- *Domestic Relations Mediation* — Sara Childs Grebe, Martin Kranitz & Catherine G. Crockett, Starting Your Own Mediation Practice: A Workbook (1985); Jay Folberg & Alison Taylor, Mediation: A Comprehensive Guide to Resolving Conflicts Without Legislation (1984).
- *Arbitration* — Charles P. Nemeth, Litigation, Pleadings and Arbitration (1990).

*The author disclaims liability for any litigation arising out of the utilization of the forms in Appendix E.

CONFIDENTIALITY AGREEMENT

By signing this agreement, all parties hereto commit themselves to not disclosing information that is revealed during this session and future mediation sessions. If a party violates the nature of this contract they will be subject to the penalties of breach of contract in a lawsuit.

Mediation is a voluntary process embarked upon by both parties of free will to resolve the issues set forth, therefore this agreement is made willingly and is not agreed upon under force or coercion.

The only exception to this agreement is that it cannot be used to aid in the commission of a crime or a fraud. Further, if the parties, or any one of them, disclose plans to commit a crime, the mediator will so advise the court.

The parties hereto agree and understand the conditions of this confidentiality contract. We agree that under no circumstances will any of the information disclosed at this mediation be revealed unless laws mandating disclosure take precedence over this confidentiality agreement.

_____   _____
Party   Date

_____   _____
Party   Date

_____   _____
Mediator   Date

AGREEMENT TO MEDIATE*

This agreement sets forth the understanding of the undersigned parties and their attorney, if any, concerning the mediation services provided by _____, as a private mediator. The agreement pertains only to the matters arising during the mediation.

1. *Legal Advice*
I understand that, as a mediator, _____ offers neither legal advice nor legal counsel. I agree to obtain legal advice on any issue of interest and not to rely on the mediator for such advice. I understand that mediators are not responsible for any issues not raised by me during the course of the mediation.

2. *Confidentiality*
I understand that this mediation is (subject to the confidentiality requirements of C.R.S. Section 13-22-307 or) confidential. I understand and agree that all discussion held during the mediation shall be confidential and that the mediator who assists us in resolving our dispute shall not be called as a witness in court to testify to facts concerning or relating to the subject matter of the mediation. I also agree that I will not subpoena documents or information about our mediation which may be retained in any file belonging to the mediator. I agree that the mediator may discuss the mediation with my attorney, if any. However, nothing disclosed to the mediator in confidence by one party will be discussed with the other party, or their attorney, without their consent.

3. *Resolution*
I agree to enter into this mediation in good faith and I will sincerely attempt to resolve the issues in dispute. I understand that upon conclusion of this mediation, the mediator will draft a Memorandum of Understanding which summarizes any and all points of agreement. This Memorandum will be mailed to the parties and their attorneys, if any, for review. After being signed by all parties, their attorneys and the mediator, the Memorandum may be incorporated by reference into documents filed with the Court.

---

*Grateful acknowledgment is given to Nancy S. Greif, Attorney, Counselor at Law and Mediator, in Durango, Colorado for permitting me to use her form here.

4. Fees

I agree to pay the mediator the fees associated with this mediation and, if applicable, any interest on the unpaid balance of the account and any costs of collection.

Dated signatures of parties, party addresses and telephone numbers, and signatures of parties' attorneys.

190

Mediation Retainer Agreement*

This letter is intended as a Mediation Retainer Agreement between the two of you and me.

During our initial meeting of   I advised you that mediation is an innovative approach to the process of dispute resolution, wherein the Mediator supervises the parties' negotiations, but the parties' ultimate agreement is up to them. The Mediator's functions may be described as follows:

1. To keep your negotiations with one another moving forward;

2. To explore settlement scenarios and options for your consideration;

3. To explain in plain language certain New Jersey family law principles that may apply to the options before you; and

4. To help you articulate what you want to say, and to help you understand what the other person is trying to say.

As a Mediator, I do **not** function as an attorney in the traditional attorney–client relationship, even though I am a licensed attorney in this State. I do not represent either one of you as your individual lawyer, nor do I represent both of you as a lawyer, since to attempt to do so would represent an impermissible conflict of interest. Whenever you require specific advice and advocacy about what may be best for you individually, you should consult with your own attorney, accountant, or other adviser(s) at any time, except during mediation sessions. Such advisers are welcome to attend sessions if that arrangement is mutually agreeable to the parties or specifically requested by the Mediator.

I will maintain strict Mediator-client confidentiality, to the full extent permitted by (New Jersey) the law. However, I am required to report to the legal authorities any imminent and serious threat to the physical well-being or life of another person (including the two of you) that may come to my attention during our sessions.

---

*Grateful acknowledgment is given to Hanan M. Isaacs, Esq, Attorney and Mediator in Princeton, New Jersey, for permitting me to use his form.

I have advised you that you are required, as a condition of my agreement to provide Mediation services, to fully, fairly, honestly, and accurately disclose any and all relevant financial documents and information that may need to be exchanged between the two of you as part of your negotiations with one another. Failure to do so may result in the Court's cancellation of your agreement with one another, in whole or in part, and will result in my suspension of this process if such failure becomes known during our work together.

I also have advised each of you to retain separate (New Jersey) licensed legal counsel of your own choice to finalize any agreement that may result from your mediated negotiations. It is very important that each of you has the benefit of separate and skilled matrimonial legal counsel before signing any agreements that may result from our meetings together. I take no responsibility for your failure to retain, consult with, and/or follow the advice of such legal counsel.

My fee for the initial meeting was billed to you at $ per hour to 1.5 hours. The second session and any follow-up sessions will be charged to you at $ per hour, to be divided between the two of you 50-50, or on some other agreed-upon basis. Fees are due and payable on a "per session" basis. You also will be responsible for my time in A) conferring with either of you by telephone between in-person meetings (charged at a minimum of 1/10th of an hour per call); B) drafting all interim mediation synopsis letters; and C) drafting a final letter, called a Memorandum of Understanding. The Memorandum of Understanding will incorporate the terms of your tentative agreement with one another.

Telephone conference time and interim synopsis letters are chargeable at the session following those activities, in addition to our time together during the next session. I also will require a deposit before I draft the final Memorandum of Understanding, representing an estimate of the required hours of drafting time. Minor changes and corrections to the Memorandum will be done at no additional charge. Major rewrites will be charged at the rate of $ per hour, payable in advance.

If you jointly retain experts, such as accountants, appraisers, or the like, the two of you will be responsible to pay such expenses directly to the provider(s), and to divide the cost of such services 50/50, or on some other agreed-upon basis.

Please carefully review the terms of this letter agreement and ask me any questions that you may have about its contents. Once you are satisfied that you understand the terms set forth in this letter, please then sign the "better" original where indicated, fill in the date, and return the countersigned document to me. Your signature will signify that you have agreed to proceed according to the terms as written. The signed, enclosed copy of this letter (one for each of you) is for your own records.

If either of you needs to cancel a mediation session, please be sure to call me **at least** 24 hours in advance, except in a bona fide emergency. For cancellations upon less than 24 hours' notice, it is office policy to charge for one full hour of set-aside time, payable at the following session. Please also notify the other party of an anticipated cancellation. If a legal or personal emergency arises that requires my cancellation of a planned session, then I will give both of you as much advance notice as possible.

Thank you again for having selected me as your Mediator, and I look forward to working with both of you in this important matter.

Dated signatures of parties and mediator

MEDIATION AGREEMENT

WHEREAS, the undersigned parties to a dispute have reached the following agreements and accords, and;

WHEREAS, the undersigned parties wish to embody said agreements and accords in written form as set forth herein.

NOW THEREFORE, it is agreed that:

1. _____

_____

2. _____

_____

3. _____

_____

We, the undersigned, have read this agreement and by our signatures acknowledge that:

1. We enter it willingly and without force or coercion,
2. We have read this agreement, or it has been read to us, and we understand all the terms of the agreement,
3. We understand that this agreement is an embodiment of the compromise reached between the undersigned parties and that we will use all efforts to see that the agreement is not breached. (Alternate sentence: We agree to uphold all the terms of this agreement.)

Dated signatures of all parties and mediator.

Bibliography

American Arbitration Association & American Bar Association, Code of Ethics for Arbitrators in Commercial Disputes (1977).

American Arbitration Association, American Bar Association & Society of Professionals in Dispute Resolution, Model Standards of Conduct for Mediators (1994).

American Bar Association, Model Rules of Professional Conduct 4.1(a), 4.2(a) (1983, 1995 ed.).

Bush, Robert A. Baruch, The Dilemmas of Mediation Practice: A Study of Ethical Dilemmas and Policy Implications (National Institute for Dispute Resolution).**

Chasen, Andrea Nager, Defining Mediation and Its Use for Paralegals, 9 J. Paralegal Educ. Prac. 64 (April 1993).

Chernick, Richard, Private Judging, 3 BNA Alternative Disp. Resol. Rep. 397 (1989).

Conflict Between People & Groups (Stephen Worchel & Jeffrey A. Simpson eds., 1993).

Coulson, Robert, How to Stay Out of Court (1985).

Domenici, Kathy, Mediation: Empowerment in Conflict Management (1996).

Federal Rules of Civil Procedure 68.

Fisher, Roger, et al, Getting to Yes (2d ed. 1991).

Folberg, Jay & Taylor, Alison, Mediation: A Comprehensive Guide to Resolving Conflicts Without Litigation (1984).

Forlenza, Samuel G., Mediation and Psychotherapy: Parallel Processes, Community Mediation: A Handbook for Practitioners and Researchers (Karen Grover Duffy, James W. Grosch & Paul V. Olczak, eds., 1991).

Forum, National Institute for Dispute Resolution 11.3 (1994).

Forum, National Institute for Dispute Resolution, No. 26 (Summer 1994).

Gale, Dick S., ADR at the Crossroads, Disp. Resol. J. (March 1994).

Garrett, Robert D., Mediation in Native America, 49 Disp. Resol. J. 38 (March 1994).

Goldberg, Stephen B., Sander, Frank E. A. & Rogers, Nancy H., Dispute Resolution: Negotiation, Mediation, and Other Processes (2d ed. 1992).

**Black's Law Dictionary (6th ed. 1990).

Grebe, Sara Childs, Kranitz, Martin & Crockett, Catherine G., Starting Your Own Mediation Practice: A Workbook (1985).

Irvine, Mori, Mediation: Is it Appropriate for Sexual Harassment Grievances?, Ohio St. J. Disp. Resol. 28 (1993).

Kerr, Charles A., In Mediation What Am I?, The Alternative, Dispute Resolution Center of Snohomish and Island Counties, Everett, Washington (Spring 1993).

Kovach, Kimberlee K., Mediation, Principles, and Practice (1994).

Kruger, Judith A. & Duryea, Michelle LeBaron, The Tapestry of Culture: A Design for the Assessment of Intercultural Disputes, at 68, *in* Taking Stock, 1992 Proceedings of 20th Annual Conference of Society of Professionals in Dispute Resolution, Oct. 1992, Washington.

Lambros, Thomas, Summary Jury Trial — An Alternative Method of Resolving Disputes, 69 Judicature 286 (1986).

Leeson, Susan M. & Johnston, Bryan M., Ending It: Dispute Resolution in America (1988).

Lerman, Lisa G., Mediation of Wife Abuse Cases: The Adverse Impact of Informal Dispute Resolution on Women, 7 Harv. Women's L.J. 57, 72 (1984).

Mandated Participation and Settlement Coercion: Dispute Resolution as it Relates to the Courts, Report #1 of the Law and Public Policy Committee (1991), Society of Professionals in Dispute Resolution, Washington.

Maselko, C. James, Support/Confrontation (1980).

_____, The Fair Fight (Effective Aggression) (1985).

McEwen, Craig & Maiman, Richard J., Small Claims Mediation in Maine: An Empirical Assessment, *in* Stephen B. Goldberg et al., Dispute Resolution: Negotiation, Mediation, and Other Processes 148-155 (2d ed. 1992).

McIver, John P. & Keilitz, Susan, Court-Annexed Arbitration: An Introduction, 13 Justice Sys. J. 123 (1991).

Murray, John S., Rau, Alan Scott & Sherman, Edward F., Process of Dispute Resolution: The Role of Lawyers (1989).

Myers, Selma & Filner, Barbara, Mediation Across Cultures: A Handbook about Conflict & Culture (1993).

National Association for Legal Assistants Canons.

Nemeth, Charles P., Litigation, Pleadings and Arbitration (1990).

Raiffa, Howard, The Art & Science of Negotiation (1982).

Rowe, Mary P., The Corporate Ombudsman: An Overview and Analysis, *in* Negotiation Theory and Practice 433-434 (J. William Breslin & Jeffrey Z. Rubin eds. 1993).

Sander, Frank E. A., The Courthouse and Alternative Dispute Resolution, *reprinted in* Negotiation Strategies for Mutual Gain: The Basic Seminar of the Program on Negotiation at Harvard Law School (1993).

Scott, Gini Graham, Resolving Conflict (1990).

Singer, Linda R., Settling Disputes: Conflict Resolution in Business, Families, and The Legal System (2d ed. 1994).

Society for Professionals in Dispute Resolution, Making the Tough Calls: Exercises for Neutral Dispute Resolvers (1991).

Tractenberg, Paul L., New Jersey Dispute Resolution: A Lawyer's Guide to State and Federal Court Programs (1994).

Index